WHAT PRINCIPALS NEED TO KNOW ABOUT

Differentiated

Mobile

Instruction

SECOND
EDITION

A Joint Publication

Solution Tree   naesp

GAYLE GREGORY

Copyright © 2012 by Solution Tree Press

555 North Morton Street
Bloomington, IN 47404
800.733.6786 (toll free) / 812.336.7700
FAX: 812.336.7790

email: info@solution-tree.com
solution-tree.com

Solution Tree
Jeffrey C. Jones, CEO
Edmund M. Ackerman, President

Solution Tree Press
President: Douglas M. Rife
Publisher: Robert D. Clouse
Vice President of Production: Gretchen Knapp
Managing Production Editor: Caroline Wise
Senior Production Editor: Suzanne Kraszewski
Proofreader: Michelle Cohen
Cover and Text Designer: Jenn Taylor

TABLE OF CONTENTS

- *Leaders:* These staff members are open to change, are critical thinkers, and are respected by other faculty members.

- *Early majority:* These staff members are cautious; they will follow others if others support the innovation.

- *Late majority:* These staff members are hesitant to get involved.

- *Resistors:* These people are often opposed to new ideas. They are usually outside the "inner circle," and others often view them as negative.

These categories illustrate what principals and other school leaders have long known: some people are adaptable and amenable to trying new strategies and techniques while others are not. Their reasons for acceptance or rejection of change can come from personality differences or past experiences in the change process.

Table I.1 lists these five categories, the approximate percentage of each type of person among staff (as identified by Rogers, 1995), the characteristics, and the ways principals can support each type of personality.

Table I.1: Five Categories Related to Change

Personality Types	Characteristics	Support
Innovators (8 percent)	Eager to try new ideas and dive in; not always supported by others	Encourage innovators to blaze the trail. Provide opportunities, time, and resources to let them experiment.
Leaders (17 percent)	Critical thinkers who are open to change and are respected by faculty	Provide leaders with articles and research about differentiation. Allow for visits to other schools or classrooms, and encourage book or video studies.
Early majority (29 percent)	Cautious; will follow others if they support the innovation	Provide the early majority with collaborative time with others who are implementing the model.
Late majority (29 percent)	Reticent to get involved with the innovation	Provide time for encouragement and support from the early majority (without pressure). Provide easy strategies for the group to begin to implement and transfer.
Resistors (17 percent)	Often opposed to new ideas, outside the inner circle, and seen as negative	Provide information. Keep these staff members in the loop. Share easy strategies and materials that will provide success with students.

Source: Rogers, 1995.

By assessing teachers in relation to the five categories, principals can better understand the level of support required during implementation of differentiated instruction. However, it is important for principals not to label staff members. The categories are meant to give principals a sense of how best to support staff members as they implement differentiated instruction and how to appropriately respond to teachers' needs to keep them moving forward in the implementation process.

Staff members also might go through stages of concern as they implement any new process or adapt to a change. Hord, Rutherford, Huling-Austin, and Hall (1987) created the Concerns Based Adoption Model (CBAM) to illustrate the stages of concern. These stages relate to awareness of the initiative, how the initiative impacts an individual, what tasks are involved, and the overall impact. In these various stages, staff members will want information to know how the change affects them, how they will make time for the change, whether it will make a difference for students, and what other people are doing; finally, they will accept the task and refocus on it. These stages are useful in assessing the progression of implementation of a schoolwide change and determining what support and interventions might be helpful to move people along the continuum to complete implementation. Table I.2 shows the focus, stage, concern, and necessary support in this model.

Table I.2: Concerns Based Adoption Model—Stages of Concern and Support

Focus	Stage	Concern	Support
Awareness	Awareness	Is this another bandwagon?	Help develop the concept for staff members.
Self	Information	What is differentiation?	Provide information. Discuss in team meetings. Provide articles, and encourage book studies.
	Personal	How will this affect me?	Help people start small. Allow time for staff to see how others are doing it.
Task	Management	How will I find time? Will this cause chaos?	Create opportunities to share and solve problems. Share strategies for implementation.
Impact	Consequence	Does it make a difference for students?	Visit other teachers who are further along in implementation. Discuss the impact of the model.
	Collaboration	What are my colleagues doing?	Continue to provide team time and opportunities for support, sharing, and interaction.
	Mastery/ Refocusing	I think I can make this better. I can see a need for improvements.	Adapt innovation to suit staff needs with professional dialogue and alterations.

Source: Hord et al., 1987.

Addressing Parent Concerns

Principals must ensure that all stakeholders support the classroom changes that result from implementation of differentiated instruction—this includes parents. Parents are sensitive to change in classrooms and will need to be reassured about the advantages of using differentiation to personalize instruction. A differentiated classroom can look very different to parents—both the environment and the student work. Parents who remember sitting in rows of desks listening to the teacher and spending homework time on textbooks may be disconcerted with changes in how their children are being taught. Parents of students with special needs may be appreciative, while parents of gifted learners may be more skeptical because they might think differentiation means the school is focusing on struggling students rather than on meeting their child's needs (Tomlinson, 1999b).

Principals should consider their current relationships with parents: Are parents in the school community generally positive? How have you worked with them to resolve concerns in the past? Arroyo, Rhoad, and Drew (1999) offer the following suggestions to encourage communication and enlist parental support:

- Include parents on planning teams.

- Clearly communicate definitions and expectations for students.

- Regularly communicate with parents at the school level (principal) and at the classroom level (teachers).

- Involve parents in the classroom so that they can become comfortable with differentiation.

- Plan incremental change in classrooms to differentiate instruction.

- Provide parents with opportunities to give feedback about their concerns, and incorporate their suggestions whenever possible.

Principals must reassure parents that their child's learning needs are being better met through the highly individualized instruction of differentiation. Ongoing and regular communication is critical to build support, as is providing literature and resources about differentiated instruction (Shellard, 2002).

Making a Long-Term Commitment

Principals must recognize the importance of patience and consistency when creating changes in the school environment (Gregory, 2008). Even small changes in educational practice can take a while to become well-established routines. Implementation of a schoolwide model such as differentiated instruction requires the development of long-term goals in such areas as staffing, budgeting, developing teachers, and evaluating programs. Benchmark goals will help principals measure progress along the way. Celebrations of success provide motivation and inspiration and can incorporate opportunities for staff to share their ideas with one another. Just as schools develop plans to implement technology or a specific type of evaluation, a plan for differentiating instruction in all classes within a solid curriculum will help guide the process.

Where to Start

This book begins by offering a discussion of differentiation—what it is, what it is not, and the elements of a differentiated classroom—so principals can help staff members develop a shared definition. Then it examines the need for differentiation given what we know about how the brain works and the concept of nature and nurture, including the impact and uniqueness of prior knowledge and experience, and outlines the brain's memory processing system to shed light on why differentiation is key to the success of every learner.

Principals then learn about differentiation as it relates to student temperament, personality, and sensory-based differences; multiple intelligences; and gender and culture. Understanding the various ways that individuals learn is critical to designing instruction for all students. This allows principals to help teachers create individual student learning profiles using several tools to identify student strengths and needs, and then provide strategies learners can use to engage their strengths and compensate for their weaker areas.

An examination of how differentiation fits into a solid foundation of curriculum development and unit design addresses lesson planning, types of assessment, and how to use assessment data to plan in successful differentiated classrooms. These practices, while not unique to differentiated instruction, assist educators in successfully responding to a wide variety of learners.

Principals will also learn specific strategies to differentiate instruction in the classroom—from accommodating individual learners to differentiating instruction for the whole classroom, with a section on how technology can assist in differentiating instruction.

Classroom management is a crucial issue in the differentiated classroom; therefore, principals will also learn strategies for using time and materials effectively as well as for developing independent and interdependent learners. These strategies will help principals support teachers who are often worried that differentiation will lead to chaos in the classroom.

At the end of each chapter, reflection questions will help principals focus their efforts to support and encourage teachers and provide them with high-quality best practices for differentiation.

A Process Rather Than a Destination

Differentiated instruction is a philosophy that—if effectively embraced—creates dynamic learning environments and fosters learning for every teacher and student. A commitment to this instructional orientation requires a commitment to nurturing teachers, helping them to become masterful at differentiating instruction. It involves a commitment to many stakeholders, including students. While the process of change may sometimes seem arduous, the reward of perseverance is a high level of student success schoolwide. Principals should keep in mind that differentiation is not a destination; rather, it is a continuous process of responding to students individually and collectively and supporting teachers in this important task.

Reflections for Principals

1. How can you begin developing a plan of action to encourage differentiated instruction? What do you know about the concept, and what does the staff know?

2. What are some things you need to do immediately?

3. What would a plan for your staff look like? How will you begin?

4. What resources, materials, and people are in place already?

5. How can you help stakeholders become informed about differentiated instruction?

6. How will parents feel about the change? Staff? How do these two stakeholder groups generally respond and adapt to change?

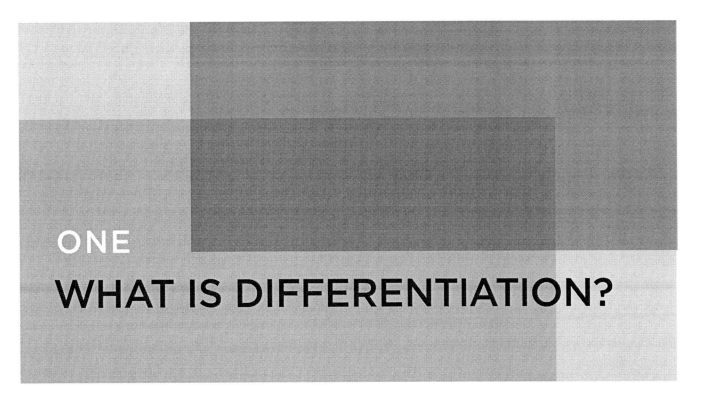

ONE
WHAT IS DIFFERENTIATION?

Differentiated instruction is "a way of thinking about the classroom with the dual goals of honoring each student's learning needs and maximizing each student's learning capacity" (Tomlinson & Eidson, 2003, p. 3). As a concept, differentiated instruction is based on what we know about the students in our classrooms, how their brains operate (similarly in many ways but that they are uniquely wired), and on the belief that students have different learning profiles. Differentiated instruction advocates that students should be active learners, decision makers, and problem solvers in the classroom. The goal of instruction is to help all students achieve their potential through precision and creative curriculum development toward targeted core standards.

Differentiation is not new. It is what good teachers have always done, often intuitively. If something is not working for students, most intelligent teachers stop doing it and try something else. We might say these teachers are "with-it" as they observe and respond appropriately to different situations. They consider such questions as the following:

- What do our students need right now?

- What must we change, stop, start, or continue?

- Who should be doing what, and with whom?

- What works best with a particular student?

- Why is a student exhibiting a particular behavior?

Real differentiation implemented over time is data driven and planned with conscious precision. It requires that principals and teachers have a mindset of growth for themselves and their students. Differentiation is *possibility thinking*.

There are many myths related to differentiation. Both teachers and parents have misconceptions about what differentiation is, and this can lead to reluctance to support the concept. Table 1.1 explains what differentiation is and what it is not.

Table 1.1: What Differentiation Is, and What It Is Not

Differentiation Is . . .	Differentiation Is Not . . .
• A mindset or philosophy • Using a toolkit of strategies as appropriate for learners and standards • Flexible grouping in a variety of ways for a variety of reasons • Proactively planned with precision, using data about students' readiness, interests, and learning profiles • A focus on quality curriculum, instruction, and assessment • Rigor and relevance for all students • Necessary for all students to achieve success and reach their potential • Evolving based on current academic and social needs • Based on clear learning objectives • Student involvement that fosters relationships and reflection • Interdependence and independence • A classroom managed with sound routines and procedures	• A new strategy • A set of strategies • Grouping students by ability • Something a teacher does or doesn't do • Only about instruction • Lowering the bar • Teaching to the middle or only for the gifted • Static • Just fun activities • Teacher directed • A chaotic environment without structure

Differentiation Defined

Differentiation is a mindset or philosophy in which the teacher knows the curriculum and standards, has an understanding of the uniqueness of his or her learners, and then—using an array of instructional approaches and assessment tools—plans with precision and flexibility to enable all students to be successful.

Developing a Shared Definition

As we know, a clear vision and purpose increases the chances of achieving any goal; therefore, it is important for principals to actively clarify the shared understanding of differentiated instruction and help staff develop a definition of the concept. If you asked each teacher individually in any one school, "What is differentiation?" you would likely get as many responses as teachers. As an administrator, it is worth taking the time to clarify the concept of differentiation, bringing consensus among staff.

What Will Teachers Differentiate?

Three classroom elements are commonly differentiated to meet individual student needs: content, process, and product (Tomlinson, 1999a).

1. *Content:* The core standards remain constant targets for students; however, students can develop competencies and big ideas (concepts) and knowledge and skills through varied content, resources, and materials that spark their interests and meet their needs, as long as it takes them to the same learning outcome stated in the curriculum.

2. *Process:* Process is how teachers teach and how students come to understand new information. The core standards are constant; the process—how students learn—is what is differentiated. Students (or groups of students) can get to the same goal in a variety of ways. In differentiated instruction, teachers provide students with a variety of learning activities to help them make sense or develop understanding. This is an opportunity for students to experience elaborative rehearsal, which is the process of moving information and skills from working memory to long-term memory.

3. *Product:* Product is how students demonstrate their knowledge of a topic or area of interest. In differentiation, there are many ways for students to process information and demonstrate their understanding or competence. These products are usually in the form of authentic culminating assessments that engage students and provide them with choices.

What Does Differentiation Look Like?

There are many pieces that make up a differentiated classroom—it is not the implementation of one strategy or idea. Some teachers implement a portion of the concept, but, like a puzzle, all the pieces must be present for the picture to be complete. Gregory and Chapman (2007) describe the following six elements of a differentiated classroom.

1. *The climate is growth oriented:* The climate in a differentiated classroom is safe and nurturing, encourages risk taking, is inclusive, appeals to all senses, is stimulating, complex, challenging, and collaborative, has a team- and class-building orientation, and includes norms for behavior.

2. *The teacher knows the learner:* In a differentiated classroom, teachers take purposeful steps to know their learners. They determine student learning profiles and become more aware of how students learn and prefer to learn.

3. *Assessment is part of the process:* In the differentiated classroom, teachers use various forms of assessment to create a picture of what each student knows, understands, and can do at different stages in the learning process.

4. *Assignments are adjustable:* In the differentiated classroom, assignments and groups are adjustable—they can be changed to meet the readiness and preferences of diverse learners.

5. *Instructional strategies are varied:* Differentiated instruction involves instructional strategies that provide a mixed-modality pedagogy (Geake, 2009) that will ultimately support students' learning needs and increase student learning. Teachers do not use a one-size-fits-all approach.

6. *A variety of curricular models are used:* These create opportunities to develop broad concepts and incorporate critical and creative thinking, such as project- and problem-based inquiry, to help move students toward mastery.

Table 1.2 lists the six elements of a differentiated classroom and specific considerations and strategies teachers might use in each category within the differentiated classroom. (Specific strategies are addressed in more depth in later chapters.)

How Do Teachers Determine Differentiation?

Sousa and Tomlinson (2011) identify three student characteristics that teachers should consider as they make decisions about what and how to teach when they are differentiating instruction:

1. *Student readiness*—This is the current knowledge and level of understanding or skills that students possess at the outset of a unit of study. Preassessments are key in determining readiness.

2. *Student interest*—This characteristic includes the topics in which students are interested and about which they enjoy learning. Engaging student interest serves as a hook to bring students into the learning and keep them engaged and motivated. Learning contracts may be developed to outline what the student must do or can choose to do related to developing competencies.

3. *Student learning profiles*—These include students' preferred modes of learning, which may be influenced by learning styles, multiple intelligences, gender, and culture. These characteristics help teachers determine the best ways to help students acquire, process, and demonstrate competencies towards targeted core standards.

Table 1.3 (page 14) shows examples of differentiation teachers can use in each of these three areas.

Supporting a Shared Definition

As mentioned previously, people usually have ideas or misconceptions about a new innovation. Staff members might possess a continuum of expertise or knowledge related to a complex topic such as differentiated instruction. They might also have concerns or question their personal competency related to implementation. As a leader, it is best to be aware of those issues so that you can respond to concerns and provide resources accordingly. To help teachers clarify the concept of differentiation, principals should take time at faculty meetings to discuss the concept. Begin by asking each teacher to share his or her beliefs about the method, preferably in a collaborative way. Principals can use the strategy of synectics or a brainstorming activity for reflection and to help build shared knowledge.

Table 1.2: The Six Elements of Differentiated Instruction

Climate Is Growth Oriented	Teacher Knows the Learner	Teacher Assesses the Learner	Assignments Are Adjustable	Teacher Uses Multiple Instructional Strategies	Approach Is Curricular
Characteristics of climate: • Safe • Nurturing • Encourages risk taking • Inclusive • Multisensory • Stimulating • Complex • Challenging • Collaborative • Involves team and class building • Has norms	Teacher gets to know the learner using: • Learning styles inventories • Multiple intelligences • Observation checklists, inventories, logs, and journals	Teacher assesses learners before, during, and after learning using formal and informal assessments such as: • Journaling • Portfolios • Surveys and inventories • Squaring off, boxing, and graffiti facts • Teacher-made tests • Checklists and rubrics • Thumb it, fist of five, and face the fact • Reflections • Talking topics • Conversation • Circles	Teacher adjusts assignments, such as by using: • Compacting • Lecturettes • Presentation • Demonstration • Jigsaw • Video • Field trips • Guest speakers • Text alone • Interest • Personalization • Multiple Intelligences • Pairing of students randomly, by interest, or by task • Small-group work (heterogeneous, homogeneous, or task oriented)	Strategies are based on: • Brain research • Multiple Intelligences • Student learning profiles Examples include: • Focus activities • Graphic organizers • Compare & contrast webbing • Metaphors • Questioning • Cubing • Cooperative group learning • Jigsaw • Role play	Approach involves broad concepts such as: • Centers • Projects • Problem-based inquiry • Learning contracts

Source: Gregory & Chapman, 2007.

Table 1.3: Differentiation in Readiness, Interest, and Learning Profile

Readiness (What is the prior knowledge or experience of the learner?)	Interest (What hooks, engages, or motivates the learner?)	Learning Profiles (What factors influence the learning?)
Preassess and structure learning with: • Layered texts • Supplementary resources • Scaffolding • Tiered tasks and products • Compacting • Peer coaching	Find or appeal to student interests by using: • Preassessments • Multiple choices • Student-generated questions • Group investigation • Negotiated tasks • Learning contracts	Consider the student's learning style: is it visual, auditory, tactile, or kinesthetic? • Provide a flexible learning environment. • Give opportunities for self-expression through multiple intelligences. • Respect cultural differences. • Consider gender issues. • Provide organizational choice. • Use agendas and learning contracts.

Synectics

William Gordon's (1961) notion of *synectics* is a creative-thinking strategy to help people make sense of a new or abstract concept by relating it to something they know well. With synectics, the brain does a compare and contrast between a well-known concept and a new or abstract one. There is no one right answer—the key is to stretch one's thinking and make connections. This process identifies the critical attributes of the new concept and uses a creative memory hook to help teachers remember it. A principal might ask his or her staff the following questions as a synectics activity to help teachers develop their understanding of differentiation, or teachers may pick their own topic for comparison:

- How is differentiation like a pizza?
- How is differentiation like flying a plane?
- How is differentiation like a box of chocolates?
- How is differentiation like a river?

Principals can facilitate this activity using small-group brainstorming with a large sheet of chart paper to record the ideas of the larger group. Often this process helps people flesh out a full picture of the facets of differentiation. It can also reveal the attitudes staff members have about differentiation. For example, a principal might ask staff members to choose their own object for comparison with differentiated instruction. One reluctant group chose to compare differentiation to a train wreck. This was valuable information about how they viewed the concept, and it helped the principal understand the group's apprehension about the approach and then address the group's concerns.

Brainstorming Activity

A brainstorming activity is another strategy principals can use to assess the understanding of differentiation among staff members and address their concerns. For this activity, divide a piece of chart paper into four parts (four corners), each part with a different heading (as shown in figure 1.1), and ask the group to brainstorm ideas for each corner.

Create a symbol or drawing to represent differentiation.	What is something you already do to respond to different learners in your classroom?
Brainstorm words related to differentiation.	What is your greatest apprehension about differentiated instruction?

Figure 1.1: Four corners for differentiated understanding.

Examining Mindset

From working with teachers to develop a shared understanding of differentiation, principals may discover that people view intelligence, ability, and success in different ways. According to Carol Dweck (2006), a researcher and Stanford psychology professor, individuals' opinions fall along a continuum with *fixed* on one end and *growth oriented* on the other.

Those who believe their success depends on hard work and learning are said to have a *growth* mindset (also known as a *fluid* mindset). These people are more likely to persist even with setbacks. They actually believe that they can improve their success if given other opportunities. Those who believe that they are born with a limited ability are described as having a *fixed* mindset. These people are more likely to fear failure because it reinforces their limited capabilities. They believe they have personal limitations and thus give up when not immediately successful. Effective teachers are said to have positive growth mindsets that affect their behavior in the classroom (Brooks & Goldstein, 2008). Studies show that "children raised in growth-mindset homes consistently outscored their fixed-mindset peers in academic achievement. They do better in adult life too" (Medina, 2010, p. 140).

Children's mindsets, according to Dweck (2006), also develop as a result of their educational and classroom experiences and interactions. In the classroom, a student's mindset about whether or not he or she can be successful is reinforced or revised based on subtle—or not so subtle—comments about the student's performance. When a teacher praises a student by saying something such as, "Wow, you are really smart!" he or she validates a fixed mindset.

In contrast, comments and encouragement such as, "Good job! I see you are working hard!" may help students develop a growth mindset. The second statement encourages the student to persist.

Some elements of traditional school curricula may actually reinforce a fixed mindset for students, such as the use of standardized testing that shows only what students know at one point in time and with one form of measurement. Students who fail to show progress on these tests may be apathetic and frustrated by the time they reach middle school. "Why bother?" a student might think, "I'll always be a failure." Differentiated instruction can combat this mindset and encourage a growth mindset because learning differences are celebrated—teachers provide a variety of ways to learn, and they acknowledge that each learner learns in his or her own way, in his or her own time.

Encourage Reflection

Part of the principal's role is to foster his or her staff members' reflective thinking skills so that self-reflection becomes daily routine practice. This will help teachers continue to increase their skillfulness in the classroom with differentiated instruction. Ask teachers to take a moment to reflect on their own mindset about learning. Ask them the following questions:

- Do you believe that students' abilities are predetermined by genetics, experiences, and their home environment?

- Do you believe that some students will not be able to learn?

- Do you believe that every student can learn this year?

- Do you believe that every child can achieve success with hard work, multiple opportunities, persistence, and a variety of instructional approaches offered by the teacher?

Teachers with a fixed mindset regarding who can learn and who has potential might have limited abilities to effectively apply differentiated instructional strategies. Teachers who have a growth mindset will stay motivated to seek out and implement a variety of learning opportunities for all students. Thus, teachers with a growth mindset are more likely to be successful because they have high expectations and an optimism of success.

There are ways for principals to help teachers develop a growth mindset. They can explore success stories with faculty members by reading stories and watching movies, both biographical and fictional. For example, the movie *Freedom Writers* shows how one teacher successfully motivates a group of teens in Long Beach, California, when the rest of the system and community had labeled them as failures with no hope for success. The movie *Mr. Holland's Opus* allows viewers to see how a teacher can adjust his or her methods based on learner needs rather than just giving up.

Summary

Creating a schoolwide definition of differentiated instruction that is generated and validated by everyone on the faculty creates shared direction and understanding. This kind of shared understanding allows leaders, staff, teachers, parents, and students to be on the same page. Encouraging teachers to view student learning with a growth mindset will help the concept of differentiated instruction take hold so that it is a part of every classroom.

Reflections for Principals

1. Is there a shared understanding of the concept of differentiation among the faculty?

2. Are teachers able to articulate their shared understanding?

3. Do faculty members have input into clarifying the vision and plan for implementing differentiated instruction?

4. Are teachers comfortable talking about their mindset—the expectations that they share for students and the learning in their classroom?

5. Is there a growth mindset among teachers and students in our building? If not, how can you work toward changing the fixed mindset to one of growth?

TWO

WHY DO WE NEED DIFFERENTIATION?

We know that every person is unique—a product of nature and nurture—and that our varied environments and experiences contribute to what we know and how we learn. Genetics do play a role in brain growth and development, but many neuroscientists believe that environmental factors may be an even greater influence (Shaw et al., 2006). Consider, for example, that identical twins have differently wired brains (Medina, 2008). Indeed, as Howard Gardner (2006) suggests, brains are as individual as thumbprints. However, thumbprints remain the same—unchanged throughout a lifetime. Brains, on the other hand, change. Brain growth—connections between neurons—continue throughout life and into old age (Kandel, Schwartz, & Jessell, 2000).

Given this information, it is logical and reasonable to expect that no one way of teaching students is *the right way* for all. Differentiated instruction is an approach to reaching and teaching the diverse students in our classrooms today. The rationale for differentiated instruction comes from brain research.

Examining Brain Research

Understanding how the brain works helps educators create the classroom conditions and offer the learning experiences that most benefit learners. Following are some things we know about the brain and how differentiated instruction supports each point.

The brain seeks patterns and schemas to make sense of the world. It decides if things are meaningful and how they relate to what we already know, and meaningful information is stored in our long-term memory. Differentiated instruction creates patterns in a variety of ways, from social interaction to visual, auditory, and tactile and kinesthetic activities.

The human brain can engage in *convergent* thinking (such as applying knowledge to solve a problem in a particular way). This differs significantly from the traditional "sit, get, and spit" model of instruction promoted in classrooms as preparation for standardized testing. *Divergent* thinking allows learners to apply creativity to the learning process. Differentiation provides many ways to support this creativity with flexibility in the learning process.

In order for learning to take place, a learner must be able to focus his or her attention. The brain focuses on what is novel, meaningful, and relevant, and on what evokes emotions. In a differentiated setting, teachers take into account students' interests and preferences to better engage their attention. This increases student motivation, which helps students move forward in the learning process, paves the way to self-directed learning, and supports an intrinsic desire to learn. Each brain is equipped with what Panksepp (2004) calls a *seeking device*, which creates and sustains curiosity. When we find what we seek, dopamine (a neurotransmitter) is released and we feel pleasure and elation; thus, curiosity and success in the intellectual process are rewarded in the brain.

The human brain is social; we learn from others as we listen and observe their behavior. Differentiated instruction is highly social. It involves dialogue, positive reinforcement, feedback, and cooperation. Hallowell (2011), in his book *Shine*, suggests that if we are denied human interaction, we actually lose brain cells, so social interaction actually fosters brain growth.

Positive emotions play a key role in learning. A positive, satisfying learning moment releases endorphins (feel-good neurotransmitters), which help to punctuate long-term memory. The brain loves novelty and variety, which capture attention and impact retention. When teachers differentiate, they build novelty and variety into the curriculum. Learners are rewarded with a feeling of success when challenged. Humor also can enhance learning through the release of endorphins (Geake, 2009).

Negative emotions block learning. For learning to take place, learners must feel included and supported by their teacher and peers. People cannot perform higher-order processing when stress hormones are present. Stress and fear cause a learner's cerebral cortex (the thinking and rational brain area) to no longer function normally—rather, it is in survival mode in which limited language and thought processing takes place. This is the fight-or-flight reflex response (LeDoux, 2002; Posner & Rothbart, 2007; Zull, 2002).

Therefore, a positive, interesting, and emotionally supportive classroom is key for the success of all learners (Willis, 2006, 2008, 2010). A differentiated classroom is a safe atmosphere that supports risk taking and experimental thinking. Differentiated classrooms encourage trial and error without negativity or ridicule. Students need this type of environment to flourish, as do adult learners, including teachers and administrators.

Learning Is Memory Making

When students learn, they are acquiring new information or developing new skills and storing them in memory. The memory processing system consists of the following three parts: (1) sensory memory, (2) short-term (working) memory, and (3) long-term memory.

Sensory Memory

All information that enters the human brain comes from the senses: sight, hearing, touch, taste, and smell. Signals from our senses travel to the appropriate part of the brain where the sensory stimuli are perceived. Sensory memory contains a great deal of information, which is held for a very brief time and then forgotten. People ignore most sensory information because remembering every small detail would be overwhelming.

Why the brain acknowledges one signal and not another is not completely understood. It is known, however, that an individual is more likely to pay attention to:

- Information that has some personal connotation

- Sensory information that is unusual or different from the norm

- Information that is unusually intense or involves movement

In addition, some people are able to recall information better using particular senses. Differentiated instruction appeals to the sensory memory because it targets the senses with its focus on visual, auditory, and tactile and kinesthetic learning and makes personal connections with learners through their interests and learning styles.

Short-Term/Working Memory

Once the brain decides to focus on something that is interesting, relevant, or meaningful, it holds the information in short-term or working memory. While sensory memory holds abundant data for a short period of time, the working memory of most people holds about twenty seconds of information (without practicing the information). That is enough memory to keep track of what people are saying and decide whether or not to remember it.

Some learners may need up to twenty-four rehearsals to achieve 80 percent mastery (Marzano, Pickering, & Pollock, 2001). Most students don't want to practice the same way all the time. Differentiated learning provides variety by extending working memory with methods such as *chunking* (grouping information into easily remembered bits) and *elaboration* (connecting what needs to be remembered to something already known or rehearsed in novel ways). Elaborative rehearsal practices should be varied to allow a variety of different neural pathways to be formed. Incorporating the multiple intelligences into the rehearsal process provides that variety.

Long-Term Memory

Learners make long-term or permanent memories by rehearsing information, writing, associating the material with material they already know, or employing numerous other techniques. *Declarative memory*—content, facts, big ideas, and concepts in the long-term memory—is affected by learning-style differences. Differentiated instruction ensures that students receive multiple opportunities to store information in long-term memory accurately and thoroughly. "Teach, test, and hope for the best" is not the goal of differentiation. Rather, teachers provide multiple opportunities to practice with a variety of engaging activities so that students make connections to the learning and increase the chance of committing important learning to the long-term memory.

Every Brain Is Uniquely Wired

Vygotsky (1978) suggests that all learners have different levels of readiness. These levels differ because of genetics, environment, prior knowledge, and experience. Some students have a higher level of readiness because they may have experienced a richer environment in their formative years, giving them a head start for new learning. Others might have had limited experiences and opportunities and may need help with prior knowledge and experience to bring them toward the targeted standard.

Differentiated instruction engages the learner at his or her zone of proximal development where the learner is neither bored nor threatened—what is known as an atmosphere of *relaxed alertness* (Caine & Caine, 1994). In this state of optimal engagement—also known as *flow* by Csikszentmihalyi (1990)—the following conditions exist:

- Challenge and skill level are well matched

- Choice and options are available

- There is an intrinsic sense of satisfaction

- Feedback is ongoing

- Time goes by unnoticed

- The learner is in a learning groove

- Students are inspired to persevere

Differentiated instruction puts students in a state of optimal engagement. It appeals to what students are interested in, and thus, it will hold their attention longer. This increases students' desire and persistence in completing or mastering tasks and acquiring knowledge.

The Learner's Sweet Spot

The term *sweet spot* comes from baseball. The sweet spot on the bat is the spot where, if the ball connects to the bat, the player will hit a home run. In the classroom, the learner's sweet spot is that distinctive place that can make all the difference in learning (Gregory & Kaufeldt, 2012). All learners have a sweet spot—the point at which their attention, interests, positive feelings, and prior successes come together to make them primed for optimal learning. The sweet spot is where crystallization of learning occurs. Damasio (2003) calls this *maximal cognitive efficiency*. Figure 2.1 shows the learner's sweet spot.

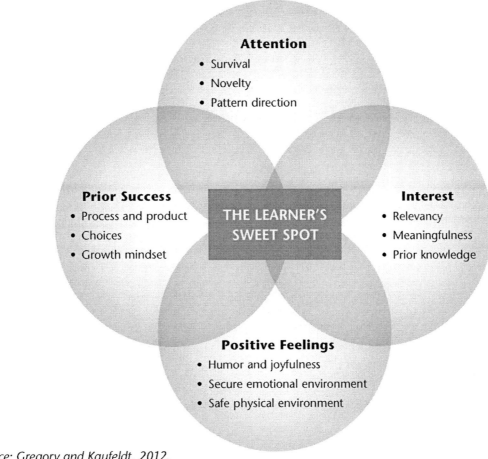

Source: Gregory and Kaufeldt, 2012.

Figure 2.1: The learner's sweet spot.

Differentiated learning targets the learner's sweet spot by creating a safe and secure learning environment; appealing to students' unique abilities, interests, prior knowledge, and readiness; providing positive reinforcement and feedback; and engaging the learner so that he or she ultimately achieves success.

Summary

Brain research supports the use of differentiation—it helps educators understand why varying learning experiences benefits learners. When students are engaged in their zone of proximal development where they are neither bored nor threatened—when they are in an atmosphere of relaxed alertness—they are ready for optimal learning. Teachers can then target their students' sweet spot and help them transfer their learning into long-term memory.

Reflections for Principals

1. Are your classrooms brain friendly? What evidence do you see, hear, and feel?

2. Does the environment support risk taking and experimentation?

3. Are tasks developmentally appropriate and not one size fits all?

4. Are learning activities engaging and novel?

5. Are students comfortable and enjoying learning? Do teachers know how to find their students' sweet spot?

THREE

DETERMINING STUDENT LEARNING PROFILES

There is limited research in the field of neuroscience to support the idea that individuals learn in different ways by using different neural pathways to undertake similar tasks; however, the field of cognitive psychology tends to perpetuate the notion that learners have different *styles* that dominate their learning. Geake (2009) suggests that while most brains follow a normal developmental trajectory, each is also idiosyncratic in its strengths and weaknesses for learning particular types of information.

Learning preferences describe what individual students need in order to learn best, considering the influence of background, interests, learning styles, multiple intelligences, gender, and culture. The term *learning style* refers to the way the brain perceives and processes what it needs to learn. This is influenced by personality, psychological traits, social behaviors, developmental differences, communication styles, and environmental preferences (Ramsay, 1991). A *learning profile* includes how teachers collect, identify, and share the ways in which each student perceives, takes in, and processes information and learns best as an individual, which includes learning preferences and styles.

When teachers tailor their teaching strategies to students' learning styles and preferences, students will respond with the optimism they had when they first entered kindergarten. Students will enter learning experiences with more confidence and connectedness and will become active participants in their learning (Willis, 2007).

This chapter examines the many preferences and learning styles that make up a student's learning profile. By being aware of these preferences, teachers can better differentiate instruction for diverse learners by providing a variety of learning experiences, instruction, resources, and assessments that might appeal to them. Principals have the responsibility of encouraging teachers to create their students' profiles and respond to the data they present.

Elements of a Learning Profile

There are many variables to how students learn that impact a student's learning profile. It is also important to recognize that profiles are dynamic and evolve as students grow and change. These variables fit into six areas: student interests, sensory-based differences, differences in learning styles, differences in multiple intelligences, gender differences, and cultural differences.

1. *Student interests:* Students may have strong emotions that generate high interest based on their individual seeking system. This interest may be because of prior experience or knowledge or just because of an innate curiosity about the topic. It often generates opportunities for extended study of the topic and deepens the development of critical and creative thinking skills.

2. *Sensory-based differences:* Students have preferences based on how they best process information through their senses. Sensory source preferences include auditory, visual/verbal, visual/iconic, and kinesthetic and tactile. By designing instruction to appeal to students' sensory differences, teachers can avoid the disconnect many students experience in the classroom when they have difficulty acquiring information through a particular sense.

3. *Differences in learning styles:* These styles consider whether a student is analytic, emotional, pragmatic, and expressive, describing students' likes and dislikes and what they need for optimal learning.

4. *Differences in multiple intelligences:* Not all children are strong in all skills. Gardner (1999) describes eight intelligences—verbal-linguistic, musical-rhythmic, logical-mathematical, visual-spatial, bodily-kinesthetic, intrapersonal, intrapersonal, and naturalistic—and the skills students with strengths in each area would possess and what they need from their teachers to help them access academic material.

5. *Gender differences:* Boys' and girls' brains are different, and boys and girls have different needs in the learning process (Gurian, Henley, & Trueman, 2001).

6. *Cultural differences:* It is important to acknowledge that all students—regardless of ethnicity—have cultural differences that influence their learning, behavior, and attitudes towards school and learning.

Every student has unique preferences for learning. For example, many students are successful in classrooms that emphasize verbal skills, while others excel when movement is involved in learning. When students' learning preferences differ from the teacher's methods for instruction and presenting knowledge, it can create a barrier to learning. For students who have difficulty with more traditional approaches to instruction, teachers' efforts to differentiate and diversify their teaching methods can lead to increased student attention and engagement.

Although there are no immediate data that show learning preferences make a quantitative difference in student learning, several sources support the notion in terms of both engagement for learning and attitude toward school. Sternberg, Torff, and Grigorenko (1998) note that students who learn and express their learning in their preferred learning modes outperform students who do not have that opportunity. Sullivan (1996) confirms that addressing a student's learning style results in improved achievement and attitude in students from a wide range of cultural groups.

It is important to note that compiling a learning profile is not about labeling students; rather, it is about recognizing that students have different needs. If teachers are going to take the time to build a learner's profile, they should actually respond to the learner's preferences and needs. If they do not respond to the data, then there is no reason to compile the profile. By identifying and recognizing these needs, school leaders and teachers can ensure that learners are content and that they have what they need to increase their chances of success. All students do better with parameters, structure, and routine. Some students need precise structure to feel comfortable and some need it because they need help with organization and time management. Thus, recognizing different learning preferences helps to provide students with balance. It is also an opportunity for students to learn and value the differences in others; this helps them discover that others have strengths that can complement their own.

Student Interests

The more educators know about their students, the more they can connect learning with the individual. While it is important for teachers to get to know an individual student's interests, it is also important for students to get to know one another's interests and reflect on their own interests. The more students know, the more they can advocate their needs and respect the needs of others. Teachers can use an All About Me chart (as shown in figure 3.1) to compile information about student interests.

My family . . .	My pets . . .	My hobbies and talents . . .
I really like . . .	Outdoors, I like to . . .	Games I like include . . .
If I had a day off school to do anything I wanted . . .	I'm good at . . .	I'm working on . . .

Figure 3.1: Sample All About Me chart.

Principals can use a similar chart with teachers to learn about their personal interests. Teachers often find out many things about themselves and others with this exercise, and they realize the value of having personal information about student interests. Teachers discover what they have in common with their colleagues and how they could pique students' interests by appealing to their areas of personal interest.

Sensory-Based Differences

All incoming information to the brain originates from the senses. Most individuals have preferences for sensory sources that result in an inclination to focus on certain types of sensory information. One learning model (Dunn & Dunn, 1992) classifies learning styles through the senses: auditory, visual/verbal, visual/iconic, and kinesthetic and tactile.

1. *Auditory learners* remember what is said, learn from what the teacher says, learn from talking with other students, and appreciate the sound of their own voice.

2. *Visual/verbal learners* remember what is read and learn from reading and writing.

3. *Visual/iconic learners* remember what is seen and learn from demonstrations and videos.

4. *Kinesthetic and tactile learners* remember what is manipulated or touched and learn from doing projects and working with materials.

For example, a student who is a visual learner may have trouble understanding information a teacher presents in a lecture or in written form. The student would be able to better understand and recall information using a more visual approach, such as webbing or by presenting information on a whiteboard.

Educators should strive to help students understand their individual learning style so that they can independently increase their own possibilities for learning. The school's learning specialist can also help students identify their sensory preference and assist them in discovering approaches to the learning process based on their style. There are many surveys and inventories available online. Visit **go.solution-tree.com/leadership** to find links to several resources.

Differentiated instruction calls for teachers to vary their instruction to include all four sensory styles. Table 3.1 provides some examples of ways to differentiate instruction for students with each sensory preference, which is less about individualizing instruction and more about consciously building in opportunities for all senses to be included in the learning process.

Table 3.1: Examples of Differentiated Learning for the Four Types of Sensory Learners

Sensory Preference	How to Support the Learner
Auditory learners: Remember what is said by others and themselves	• Arrange desks so students are facing one another for face-to-face interaction. • Use phonics (sound out loud) to help with spelling and reading. • Use jokes, riddles, and tongue twisters to present material. • Use spelling bees and trivia games. • Ask students to read the text or information out loud. • Encourage students to talk while writing. • Encourage students to read papers out loud while proofreading. • Teach students to use rhymes, mnemonics, or songs to recall material. • Use language such as, "It sounds to me like . . ."
Visual/verbal learners: Remember what they read or see	• Assign students to write reports. • Teach students to read the text (especially in math). • Use lists to organize material for learning. • Engage students in dictionary or vocabulary games. • Provide students with handouts or graphic organizers to use when studying. • Write out the steps required to solve a problem. • Use sticky notes to highlight key words and concepts. • Encourage students to keep a journal or diary. • Use language such as, "The way I see it is . . ."
Visual/iconic learners: Remember what they see	• Incorporate the use of educational computer software into lesson plans. • Ask students to make a collage of visual images that tell a story. • Use colored files to store homework and papers. • Present historic material or events in a story on a timeline. • Encourage students to use symbolic representation for note taking. • Encourage students to use highlighters to color code information. • Allow students to mark up margins of a book with key words, symbols, and diagrams. • Use graph paper to create charts and diagrams. • Teach students to draw pictures and mind maps to remember facts. • Have students use flashcards.
Kinesthetic and tactile learners: Remember what they manipulate or touch	• Teach students to work with small parts of text at a time. • Use checklists to indicate when tasks are completed. • Encourage students to design a game using information from a story. • Encourage students to store homework in large colored envelopes. • Ask students to turn their paper sideways to use the lines to maintain proper columns in math. • Create note-taking booklets. • Encourage students to shift frequently between tasks, find new partners, and move into small groups. • Use four-corner discussion groups in which students move to the corner of their choice or based on their competency or agreement with a statement. • Construct models and structures. • Ask students to act out a portion of a play, book, or event. • Ask students to create actions for vocabulary words or concepts and processes.

Differences in Learning Preferences

In *Differentiated Instructional Strategies: One Size Doesn't Fit All,* Gregory and Chapman (2007) discuss four learning style preferences compiled from several theorists (Gregorc, 1985; Kolb, 1984; McCarthy & McCarthy, 2006; Silver, Strong, & Perini, 2000). These four similar learning-style preferences are analytical, emotional, pragmatic, and expressive.

1. *Analytical:* Analytical learners are detail oriented. They are often described as idea people. They prefer research and investigation, prefer to work independently, want to achieve a depth of understanding, and are logic based. They might ask questions or make statements such as:

   * "I'd like to check that out."
   * "Is that always true?"
   * "Who says so?"
   * "Do I have to work with the group?"

2. *Emotional:* These learners like to share their feelings and perspectives. They want to interact with others. They empathize with and support others and seek support in return. They crave a safe environment, and they appreciate feedback and recognition. They might ask questions or make statements such as:

   * "Can I work with a partner?"
   * "I like to work in a group."
   * "What do you think about . . . ?"
   * "I feel that . . ."

3. *Pragmatic:* Pragmatic learners like details, organization, and step-by-step learning. They do not like surprises. They prefer structure, clear procedures, consistent routines, clear expectations, and predictability. They might ask questions or make statements such as:

   * "When is the assignment due?"
   * "How much is it worth?"
   * "Do you have a rubric?"
   * "You never told us that!"

4. *Expressive:* These learners like to have a choice of activities, a variety of resources, a flexible environment, freedom, and spontaneity. They might ask questions or make statements such as:

   * "I'd rather do . . ."
   * "Do we have to . . . ?"

- "I have an idea. Instead, can we . . . ?"
- "Let's try . . ."

Table 3.2 (page 32) shows the four learning style preferences, comfort levels for each, dislikes, and what teachers should provide in the learning environment to satisfy these learners.

Principals can facilitate an activity with teachers in which participants identify their own dominant learning preference. A fun way to do this is to assign a corner of the room for each style using a picture to represent each dominant style: a microscope for analytical learners, a puppy for emotional learners, a clipboard for pragmatic learners, and a beach ball for expressive learners (Gregory & Chapman, 2007). After discussing their preferences, comfort levels, and dislikes, teachers can identify their dominant style and go to the corner of the room where their symbol is displayed. This is an active, social, and fun way to show the diversity within the staff and also respect staff members' different learning preferences. When they meet in the corners, teachers can create a list of what they appreciate as a learner and what frustrates them. It's a novel and fun way to process this information and also raise awareness that although we have similarities in how our brains learn, we also have preferences and differences as to how that learning should take place and what ensures the greatest success.

Teachers can repeat this same activity with their students to identify students' learning preferences, or they can simply observe their students—what do students say, and what do they enjoy doing in the classroom? Gregory (2005) and Gregory and Chapman (2007) have additional inventories available for identifying student learning preferences. Visit **go.solution-tree.com/leadership** to find links to various inventories.

Differences in Multiple Intelligences

Gardner (1983) proposes the concept of multiple intelligences in his book *Frames of Mind: The Theory of Multiple Intelligences*. He suggests that being intelligent is the ability to handle crises, solve problems, and create things of value for one's culture, and that intelligence is not a singular, fixed thing but rather is made up of multiple elements. Gardner's multiple intelligences model has eight intelligences: verbal-linguistic, musical-rhythmic, logical-mathematical, spatial, bodily-kinesthetic, intrapersonal, interpersonal, and naturalistic. He recognizes that there may be others (existentialist intelligence, for example). (Gardner [1999] considers the moral intelligence as the ninth intelligence, which shows concern for the processes that govern humans—a clear sense of the greater good and of right and wrong.) Gardner maintains that all individuals have these intelligences to a greater or lesser extent. Unlike a fixed fingerprint, he suggests that intelligences can grow and that an individual's profile will change with opportunities for growth or stimulation in each area.

Table 3.3 (page 33) provides a description of each intelligence, the associated skills, and suggestions for tapping into that intelligence in the classroom.

Table 3.2: Four Learning-Style Preferences

Preferences	Comfort Levels	Dislikes	Learning Environment Accommodations . . .
Analytical learners: Detail-oriented idea people	• Like to research and investigate • Prefer to work independently • Desire depth of understanding • Logic based	• Surface learning • Too much cooperative learning • Emotions rather than facts • Open-ended activities	• Expert and ample resources and references • Opportunities to work independently • Time for thorough investigation • Information provided in a timely manner • Opportunities for application and abstract thinking
Emotional learners: Lead with their feelings and want to share perspectives	• Like to socialize • Want to interact with others • Empathize with others • Support others and receive support in return • Like a safe environment • Appreciate feedback and recognition	• Isolation • Lack of emotional connection to learning • Negative tone in the classroom	• Time to work with others • Time for self-reflection • Connections with teacher and peers • Personal attention and support • Collaborative, risk-free environment • Opportunities for open communication
Pragmatic learners: Very organized—need details and step-by-step procedures	• Want step-by-step learning • Thrive with organization and structure • Need clear closure and procedures • Desire consistent routines and clear expectations • Want predictability	• Surprises • Ambiguity • Lack of organization and structure • Too many choices	• Real experiences • Concrete examples rather than just theories • A structured, orderly environment • Clear directions and models • Hands-on experience • A consistent and efficient classroom • Guided practice and feedback
Expressive learners: Flexible and spontaneous	• Like choice of activities • Want a variety of resources • Desire a flexible environment with spontaneity • Appreciate manipulatives • Want open-ended learning activities • Like personal freedom	• Lack of variety • Predictability • Repetitive tasks • Lack of choice • Lack of opportunity for expression	• Choices and variety • Opportunities for self-direction and expression • Constructive competition • Trial-and-error learning • Creative activities • Open-ended tasks and projects • Hands-on materials and resources

Table 3.3: Gardner's Multiple Intelligences

Intelligence	Skills	Learning Environment Accommodations . . .
Verbal-linguistic learners: Display an affinity for written and spoken words	Listening and speaking	• Poetry • Plays • Story writing • Note taking • Interviews • Oral reports
Logical-mathematical learners: Display an affinity for patterns, numbers, symbols, and relationships	Reasoning, logic, problem solving, and numerical thinking	• Charts and graphs • Graphic organizers • Debates • Analyzing • Problem-based assignments
Visual-spatial learners: Display an affinity for colors, shapes, and orientation	Painting, sculpting, decorating, arranging, and architecture	• Mind maps • Videos • Pictures • Diagrams • Visualizing • Posters
Musical-rhythmic learners: Display an affinity for rhyme, rhythm, and pitch/tone	Performing, composing, recognizing music, and music appreciation	• Raps or songs • Rhythm and chant • Choral reading
Bodily-kinesthetic learners: Display an affinity for using body cues and movement	Body movement of either large or small muscles	• Drama • Role play • Gallery walks • Skits • Charades • Signing • Manipulatives
Interpersonal learners: Make personal connections to others	Reading to others, responding to social cues, and collaboration	• Cooperative groups • Interviewing • Tutors/buddies • Reciprocal teaching
Intrapersonal learners: Are reflective and thoughtful and have emotional awareness	High self-concept and self-knowledge, highly self-directed, and in control of impulses	• Metacognition • Independent work • Logs or journals • Goal setting • Affirmations • Autobiography

continued →

Naturalistic learners: Are nurturing and relate information to the natural surroundings	Gardening, landscaping, and categorizing animals	• Classifying • Sorting • Predicting • Adaptation • Investigation • Analysis

There are many learning inventories available online that can be used to self-assess multiple intelligences—both with students and adults.

Many teachers have found that using the concept of multiple intelligences as a basis for planning instruction enables them to reach students who might otherwise be neglected by more traditional instruction, which is usually aimed at students who are strong in the verbal-linguistic and logical-mathematical intelligences. By adding activities designed to draw on skills associated with the other intelligences, teachers can reach more students with their instruction and provide a broader range of instructional opportunities to all students.

Principals should emphasize to teachers that differentiation using multiple intelligences is not about catering to student strengths; rather, it's about recognizing that educators must provide a full range of activities that include all eight intelligences so that at some time students are learning in ways that are most comfortable to them in a state of flow and at other times they are stretching themselves.

Table 3.4 gives suggestions for differentiating instruction in each of the intelligences.

Choice Boards

A choice board is one tool teachers can create and use to differentiate instruction based on the multiple intelligences. Principals can facilitate the process of creating these tools at a faculty meeting, and then department or grade-level teams can use the strategy at their team meetings to plan upcoming units. Choice boards give students different options for demonstrating their learning. Each board provides students with eight projects to choose from: a strategy from a different intelligence in each box. Teachers can also incorporate different levels of thinking, such as applying, analyzing, and evaluating. The assignments should focus on standards, skills, and concepts targeted in the curriculum. Start with a blank board as shown in figure 3.2 (page 37).

The completed choice boards in figures 3.3 and 3.4 (pages 37–38) show how students can rehearse content or skills related to a topic using various intelligences. Each box has a task representing one of the intelligences in it. Students select three projects (in a row) to complete. The wild card in the middle is a free choice—students may choose any task on the board or do a different (approved) task. Choice is a very successful tool for motivation and engagement.

Table 3.4: Activities for Differentiating Instruction Using the Multiple Intelligences

Verbal-Linguistic	Musical-Rhythmic
• Preparing a speech • Writing an editorial • Brainstorming ideas • Describing • Summarizing • Creating an advertisement • Developing a book • Skimming and scanning • Writing and delivering a news flash • Identifying attributes • Developing a political platform • Creating a main character with details • Researching and reporting • Creating a challenging question • Developing analogies • Identifying main and supporting ideas	• Creating a rap • Writing a song • Writing a poem • Developing a jingle or slogan • Creating sounds to go with a task • Deciding on sound effects for a presentation • Creating a beat • Using rhythmical movements • Recording music • Developing expertise with an instrument • Interpreting mood with music
Logical-Mathematical	**Visual-Spatial**
• Creating a timeline • Developing a television show • Sequencing events or items • Categorizing • Developing a process • Ranking ideas • Classifying items • Using a matrix • Creating a graph • Exploring technology • Interpreting data • Using deductive thinking • Using numbers in thinking • Solving problems using logic • Designing a survey • Displaying data • Using inductive thinking	• Using pictures and symbols • Using graphs and charts • Developing a photo essay • Making a flip book • Designing a poster • Creating a puppet • Designing a set or setting • Making a diorama • Plotting a graphic organizer • Illustrating a cartoon strip with dialogue • Using a variety of art media • Making a collage • Illustrating a story • Designing a book • Sculpting a concept • Interpreting art • Using maps, legends, and symbols • Highlighting key ideas • Illustrating a character sketch

continued →

Body-Kinesthetic	Interpersonal
• Using the body to interpret meaning	• Empathizing with others
• Miming	• Working on group projects
• Role playing	• Peer editing
• Acting	• Conducting an interview
• Using manipulatives	• Jigsawing information
• Playing a game or sport	• Being a team member
• Constructing or building	• Working with others
• Performing	• Empathizing with others
• Performing a puppet show	• Reading and discussing with peers
• Showing how you know	• Giving and receiving feedback
• Dramatizing	• Coming to consensus
• Creating simulations	• Stimulating conversation
• Designing interpretive dance	
• Doing an experiment	
• Making a model	
Intrapersonal	**Naturalistic**
• Working independently	• Using nature
• Developing logs and journals	• Studying science
• Applying metacognitive thinking	• Exploring the world
• Planning a strategy	• Applying information to life
• Making personal choices	• Making discoveries
• Setting goals	• Categorizing and classifying
• Carrying out tasks on one's own	• Noticing details
• Drawing personal conclusions and reflecting	• Observing similarities and differences
• Identifying personal preferences	• Understanding nature
• Noting personal strengths	• Developing awareness of survival needs
• Planning for working on areas of need	• Using scientific methods and classifications
	• Inventing
	• Exploring the world

Source: Gregory, 2008.

Gender Differences

The following information about gender and learning can inform teachers as they construct groups. For example, in groups, girls are often more verbal, and boys tend to be more silent. Since males have more of a need to move, teachers can include kinesthetic as well as verbal learning. Teachers can provide content and reading and writing materials that appeal to both genders to promote engagement and creativity. Helping students understand gender issues in learning and how to focus on strengths will help them recognize and be more tolerant of differences.

	Wild Card	

Figure 3.2: Blank choice board for multiple intelligences assignments.

Write and act out a new scene for the play.	Create a photo essay or brochure to chronicle the sequence of events in the story.	With a partner, act out a scene from the story. You may videotape it if you wish.
Create a theme song or rap with lyrics for the story.	Wild Card	Design a map, or paint or draw a picture of the setting.
Write a journal from the perspective of one of the characters based on the events in the story.	Write an epilogue for the story.	Finish the story with a different ending. (Did Leslie have to die? What could have happened?)

Figure 3.3: Sample choice board for *Bridge to Terabithia*, by Katherine Paterson (1977).

- Females tend to be narrow categorizers, and males tend to be wide categorizers. Narrow categorizers are better at following directions while wide categorizers are better at decision making.

- Males are typically more field independent than females—they are better able to provide an outline of material from a written source. Field-dependent students have difficulty seeing the structure from which the source was written. (It is important to note, however, that most elementary-aged children are field dependent.)

Chronicle the journey Kennedy took to the White House.	Create a timeline of key events in his presidency.	Write a news release that captures the influences Kennedy had on world history.
Write and sing a ballad that tells his story as president.	Wild Card	Investigate the music of the period and how it related to historical events. Report or present your findings.
Create an interview with at least six questions that help get at the essence of Kennedy's philosophy or intentions.	Brainstorm the key events in Kennedy's presidency and create a mind map to show them.	Design a board game to show the critical events of the presidency.

Figure 3.4: Sample choice board for a unit on John F. Kennedy's presidency.

- Males tend to think that their academic success stems from ability, whereas females tend to believe their success comes from hard work. Subsequently, boys overestimate their performance (because they know they are capable, even if they have not worked), and girls underestimate their performance (because they do not think they have worked hard enough) (Jonassen & Grabowski, 1993).

- Males demonstrate a greater visual-spatial ability than females, especially in mental rotation and spatial perception. This ability makes a difference in geometry and map-reading skills (Linn & Peterson, 1985).

- Females demonstrate greater verbal fluency, which means that they can produce more words on demand than males. Boys' vocabularies are just as large as girls', but boys are less able to supply a wide variety of words when asked by the teacher (Geary, 1998).

- Females excel at rapid access to and retrieval of information from long-term memory, whereas males excel at maintaining and manipulating a mental representation in visual-spatial working memory (Halpern, 2000). This means that females tend to excel at such tasks as language production and word fluency; computation; memory for words, objects, locations, and personal experiences; and reading comprehension and writing. Males, on the other hand, tend to excel at such tasks as verbal analogies, mathematical problem solving, spatiotemporal tasks (such as dynamic visual displays), generating and using information in visual images, and mechanical reasoning and some science-related topics (Halpern, 2000).

Cultural Differences

Appreciation of and sensitivity to cultural differences is another key part of differentiated instruction. In classrooms that are sensitive to cultural differences, the teacher demonstrates sensitivity to cultural norms, attitudes, practices, and values; encourages students to show cultural differences (and not be penalized for it); and uses materials that are culturally diverse. Being sensitive to culture helps all students feel recognized and honored. If students feel comfortable and secure, they are more likely to be able to focus on their learning. Parents are also more invested in the classroom if the teacher supports diversity and makes an effort to acknowledge students' cultural differences.

The following questions provide a starting point for teachers to develop an increased understanding of their students' cultural differences (Sileo & Prather, 1998). They help educators identify cultural practices that influence student behavior.

- What roles do silence, questions, and responses play in the students' culture?

- How do students' quiet and obedient behaviors (such as a lack of overt responding and calling attention to oneself) affect how the student learns?

- Do student behaviors result from a lack of language proficiency?

- Do students assume a competitive or a cooperative posture in their learning and interaction with other students?

- Do students put their needs and desires before those of the group, or vice versa?

- What are the students' beliefs regarding sharing belongings with others? Do these beliefs affect classroom organization and expectations?

- Do students maintain personal space or distance differentially in their interactions with other students of the same gender or opposite gender or with adults?

- What are acceptable ways to provide feedback to students about their academic performance and behaviors?

Through observation and sensitivity, teachers can consciously include cultural materials and resources in their classrooms. They can help students connect new learning by relating it to their cultures. Principals can model this approach by creating the same accepting and supportive atmosphere among the school's faculty and staff.

Summary

Knowing individual students' learning profiles is an important component of differentiation that allows for more precise instruction. By identifying students' interests, sensory-based differences, differences in learning styles, differences in multiple intelligences, gender differences, and cultural differences, educators can diagnose students' strengths and needs and develop learning plans that help students achieve success. Futurist David Thornberg used the following analogy during a lecture: When you go fishing, what do you put on the hook? The answer is, of course, bait. Not bait that *you* like, but bait that the *fish* like. If the classroom is the pond, then educators should be sure to use as many different lures and baits as necessary to "hook" all learners. Ensuring that all students participate in instructional experiences delivered through a wide variety of methods is a primary focus of differentiation.

Reflections for Principals

1. Do teachers build learning profiles of their students so they better understand students' interests, sensory-based differences, differences in learning styles, differences in multiple intelligences, gender differences, and cultural differences?

2. Do teachers provide learning experiences that appeal to students' varied learning profiles?

3. Do teachers provide instruction with ample resources, visuals, and hands-on approaches to appeal to all learners?

4. Do teachers provide opportunities for student choice within the instruction?

5. How can you further support staff members in developing their understanding of different learning styles? How can you help them build student learning profiles?

FOUR

BUILDING A FOUNDATION: CURRICULUM AND ASSESSMENT

If principals are to fully appreciate the complexities of differentiated instruction, learner differences, and how to teach to the whole class, it is important that they understand the role of curriculum and assessment in differentiation. Differentiated instruction must be built upon a foundation of solid curriculum design and assessment practice where data are used to plan with precision. This process involves identifying clear and appropriate learning standards and incorporates three types of quality assessment—preassessment, formative assessment, and summative assessment—that are built into unit design with transparency, reliability, and validity. Curricula must include tiered instruction and many opportunities for feedback from teacher, peers, and the students themselves.

Curriculum Design and Differentiation

Curriculum is influenced by national policies and standards, state standards, curriculum committees at the school or district level, and philosophical considerations related to education. The National Study of School Evaluation (1997) outlines the following indicators of a high-quality and comprehensive curriculum. A high-quality and comprehensive curriculum:

- Is based on clearly defined standards for student learning and focused on supporting and challenging all students to excel in their learning

- Includes an implementation plan that ensures alignment of teaching strategies and learning activities, instructional support and resources, and assessments of student learning

- Coordinates and articulates a shared vision for student learning held by teachers at each grade level as well as by parents and community members

- Includes a systematic process for monitoring, evaluating, and renewal, reflecting a commitment to continuous improvement

As teachers develop their unit designs, three questions should guide them (Wiggins & McTighe, 1998, p. 18):

1. *What is worthy of understanding?* Teachers should consider state and national core standards, content standards, and district curriculum standards. These then become the learning objectives or essential understanding.

2. *What is evidence of understanding?* Teachers should consider how they will assess whether the student has learned the material.

3. *What learning experiences and teaching promote understanding, interest, and excellence?* Teachers should consider how they will design lessons to best promote student understanding.

Designing units with these three questions in mind is known as *backward planning* because it begins by addressing what the student should know at the conclusion of the unit according to the standards, and how that learning will be assessed. This planning strategy helps to focus classroom instruction on meaningful learning experiences, assessment, and student understanding. Backward planning works well with differentiated instruction because adjustments for individual learners are easier for teachers to determine when they know what skills students will ultimately be expected to acquire. Once teacher teams determine the learning objectives or essential understanding, teachers can begin developing their unit assessments (Wiggins & McTighe, 1998).

Principals can support teachers with curriculum design by providing them with protected time to meet in their department or grade-level teams. They can also provide teachers with district or school and national core standards documents and staff development to examine these standards and do gap analysis between district or school standards and the core standards.

Assessment Planning and Differentiation

Assessment planning should be done before teams determine their instructional strategies and decide what learning experiences to provide to students. By creating a unit assessment at the beginning of the planning process, teams are sure to choose learning experiences and instruction that meet assessment criteria (Wiggins, 1998). Three forms of assessment—preassessment, formative assessment, and summative assessment—are key parts of curricula that involve differentiated instruction.

Preassessment

The preassessment process allows teachers to determine students' readiness levels for learning. Readiness is *not* the same thing as ability. Readiness is the prior knowledge or experience students bring to the new learning. Preassessment techniques such as K-W-L (know, want to know, learned), exit cards, quick-writes, quizzes, and graffiti boards all give quick data so teachers are aware of what students know or can do. Preassessment helps teachers plan with more precision. It can also show areas of student interests and preference that can be added to the learning profile.

Formative Assessment

Formative assessment—or assessment *for* learning—drives the learning process. These assessments inform the teacher about a student's current level of learning or mastery during the learning process. The results from this assessment provide feedback to the student about his or her progress and provide the teacher with information to determine the next steps to take in the instructional process. The results inform teachers' differentiation techniques. For example, teachers might determine how students should be grouped for upcoming learning experiences. Some examples of formative assessment include exit quick-writes, thumbs up, logs, journals, and graphic organizers.

Summative Assessment

Summative assessments—assessments *of* learning—happen once the learning is completed and are used to evaluate growth toward mastery of the standards. Teachers who provide students with opportunities to show what they know in a variety of ways—rather than always using traditional tests and quizzes—help their students learn more. Assessments that give students choices and tap into their areas of strength or interest increase students' commitment to being successful. Some nontraditional summative assessments include creating slide shows, games, videos, and brochures; writing newspaper articles, songs, and poems; conducting mock trials or debates; and compiling portfolios.

Table 4.1 (page 44) shows the three forms of assessment and gives some specific examples for each that allow for differentiation.

Elements of Quality Assessments

There are three elements of quality assessments—transparency, reliability, and validity—that principals can encourage teachers to consider as they work together in teams to create common assessments. Principals can monitor for the presence of these elements during conferencing and evaluation of teachers' planning documents.

Transparency

Transparency means that students should know what is expected of them (Frederiksen & Collins, 1989). To achieve transparency in assessment design, teachers should do the following:

- Clearly state goals and objectives at the beginning of the unit and explain the criteria for success of the task, perhaps using a rubric

- Clearly communicate what is essential to know and do for the unit assessment so students are not surprised by test questions or performance standards

- Clearly communicate with parents about the desired performance standards and how they can help their children to meet them

Reliability

Reliability means consistency in the development and grading of assessments. To foster reliability in assessment design and use, teachers should do the following:

- Preplan assessments to include model answers and the criteria by which student work is assessed

- Develop rubrics that discriminate among performance based on objective criteria, not arbitrary judgments (Wiggins, 1998)

- Develop performance criteria using descriptive language, which helps students to gauge their own performance and to make distinctions between work of different levels of quality (Wiggins, 1998)

Table 4.1: Three Forms of Assessment

Assessment	Differentiation Accommodations
Preassessment: Used to plan instruction and identify prior knowledge and experience, interests, and preferences Helps determine readiness levels	• Brainstorming • Surveys • Inventories • Quizzes • Demonstrations • Tickets out
Formative assessment: Checks for understanding throughout the learning process Provides data to modify the instructional process and feedback to the learner	• 3-2-1 cards • Exit quick-writes • Fist of five • Thumbs up • Logs • Journals • Graphic organizers
Summative assessment: Measures growth and evaluates mastery Use for grading and reporting	• Performances • Products • Projects • Models • Exhibitions • PowerPoints • Portfolios • Essays

Validity

Validity means teachers are actually measuring what they believe they are measuring. When creating assessments, teachers should do the following:

- Consider what constitutes sufficient evidence of understanding by asking questions such as, "What do I want students to know or do at the end of this unit?" and, "How can students demonstrate that they have met the learning objectives for this unit?" (Wiggins, 1998)

- Match the assessment to the appropriate learning goal or objective

- Use multiple assessments to gather enough information to accurately assess student performance

- Review the completed assessment with students to further clarify performance standards and strengths, and offer instructional support in students' areas of weakness

Feedback

There is a popular saying that feedback is the breakfast of champions. Indeed, feedback during assessment can lead to great things for students. Black and Wiliam (2009) note that if teachers put feedback on student papers—instead of a grade—students pay more attention to what they need to do to improve. Feedback propels students forward in their learning. The following guidelines will help teachers as they incorporate feedback into their assessments:

- Provide feedback to students quickly

- Allow class time for feedback and question answering

- Take advantage of the teachable moments that may appear when students provide feedback

Teachers should do the following to help students master the self-assessment and peer assessment process:

- Encourage students to discuss their understanding of performance criteria so they know when their work is exemplary, good, or substandard

- Help students to understand and value honesty

- Assist students in learning how to fairly judge another student's work

Table 4.2 outlines how assessment feedback can be differentiated according to specific student needs and behaviors.

Table 4.2: Feedback According to Specific Student Needs and Behaviors

Student Needs and Behaviors	Appropriate Teacher Feedback
Learner needs to feel in control.	• End feedback with a choice.
Learner seems confused.	• Clearly connect the current learning to the target. • Point out the parts-to-whole relationship. • Ask questions about the personal impact of the issue or task.
Learner shows anxiety with a task.	• Reduce stress by using a rubric or model so expectations are clear. • Break the steps of a task down into more achievable pieces with chunking.
Learner is easily embarrassed.	• Allow the student to choose from among a variety of acceptable methods to communicate learning in private rather than publicly.
Learner cannot get started on a project.	• Structure and limit the choices so the task seems manageable.
Learner needs frequent encouragement.	• Implement a personal checklist the student can use to self-evaluate. • Encourage language for positive self-talk. • Give specific praise that celebrates a completed goal that the student has set personally.
Learner is uncomfortable with the change in process or method.	• Give a connection to the previous process and real-world rationale for the change. • Ask the student to suggest a viable method or process that does not compromise the standard or assessment.
Learner is bored.	• Allow the student to start at a different point in the assignment or project or discuss it until the meaning is more personal for him or her.

Source: Adapted from Gregory and Kuzmich, 2004.

Principals can help teachers understand the importance of giving specific feedback and helping students self-assess. When observing in a classroom, the principal should make note of the specific feedback the teacher gives to students, the feedback students give to each other, and the feedback students achieve through self-assessment so teachers are aware of their strengths and weakness in this area.

Principals can require teachers to track how much feedback students are getting each day and from whom—their teachers, peers, or themselves (through self-assessment). Teachers can use a chart such as the one shown in figure 4.1 to note the types of feedback students have received in any of the three areas.

Teacher	Peer	Self

Figure 4.1: Chart for recording types of feedback.

Creating a Tiered Curriculum

Teachers use data from preassessments to develop a tiered curriculum that provides two, three, or four levels of learning tasks that correlate with each student's zone of proximal development or flow—what he or she can do with or without help that is challenging but not frustrating. This gives students challenges that are just beyond their skill level, creating a feeling of relaxed alertness that engages the learner but does not overstress him or her.

Tiered assignments can vary by the complexity of thinking involved, the complexity of tasks, or the complexity of content. Teachers can provide this complexity through a variety of learning experiences, such as stations, projects, or homework. Some things to remember about tiering are as follows:

- All activities should focus on the targeted core standards and content.

- All assignments should be interesting and intriguing, regardless of their level of complexity.

- Teachers should both assign tasks and allow students to negotiate the task.

For example, a tiered assignment could be one that involves three similar assignments with different degrees of support. At the beginning level, students work with assistance. At the middle level, students receive resources, and at the independent level, students find their own resources through investigation. Assignments can also be tiered by complexity or quantity, such as in the example in figure 4.2, or tiered by the student's level of readiness, as shown in figure 4.3. The three levels may also incorporate more complex technology or degrees of problem solving.

Beginning	Middle	Independent
Students will write a simple letter from a model.	Students will write a letter with three ideas to share.	Students will write a letter with five ideas to share.

Figure 4.2: Example of an assignment tiered by complexity.

Beginning	Middle	Independent
Students will work with manipulatives and place-value mats to develop an understanding of borrowing.	Students will work with a partner to solve two-digit subtraction problems with borrowing.	Students will work independently with four-digit subtraction problems using borrowing.

Figure 4.3: Example of an assignment tiered by student readiness.

Levels of Complexity and Thinking

Many educators are familiar with Bloom's Taxonomy, which classifies learning objectives into three domains: cognitive, affective, and psychomotor (Bloom et al., 1956). In 2001, Lorin Anderson and David Krathwohl revised the original taxonomy, providing new language and thus making the taxonomy more useful for educators. The revised structure now contains a taxonomy of cognitive processes that includes the categories of *remembering, understanding, applying, analyzing, evaluating,* and *creating.* This taxonomy is an important tool for teacher teams as they structure their curriculum because it is critical to go beyond just factual information to include the 21st century skills of critical and creative thinking and problem solving. These levels of thinking should be built into assignments and projects so that students are not just recalling factual information but instead are deepening their understanding by applying that knowledge in analytical and creative ways.

Table 4.3 shows the cognitive categories in the new taxonomy, the cognitive processes involved in each category, and specific verbs teachers can use in their instruction and assessment design to engage students in each category.

Table 4.3: Taxonomy of Cognitive Processes

Category	Cognitive Processes	Verbs
Remembering: Retrieving from long-term memory	• Recognize • Recall	• Identify • Retrieve
Understanding: Comprehending from words, symbols, charts, and texts	• Interpret • Summarize • Explain	• Paraphrase • Generalize • Conclude • Predict
Appyling: Using knowledge and skills	• Execute • Implement	• Use • Carry out
Analyzing: Taking apart to see components and how they relate to the whole	• Differentiate • Organize • Attribute	• Discriminate • Select • Distinguish • Determine
Evaluating: Making judgments based on criteria	• Check • Critique	• Test • Judge • Monitor • Detect
Creating: Rearranging and combining to form a new entity	• Generate • Plan • Produce	• Hypothesize • Design • Construct • Invent

Source: Adapted from Anderson and Krathwohl, 2001.

Cubing

Cubing (Cowan & Cowan, 1980) is one strategy teachers can use to draw on the different levels of cognitive processes in Bloom's (1956) and Anderson and Krathwohl's (2001) taxonomies. Cubing can be used as a processing opportunity to review and discuss material or as an assessment tool (both for oral and written assessment). In this activity, students examine a topic using a different prompt from each level of the taxonomy written on each side of a cube. The following example allows students to review and think more deeply about the concept of democracy alone, with a partner, or in a small group:

1. *Identify*—For example, define democracy.

2. *Summarize*—What are the major components of a democracy?

3. *Apply*—Connect it with something. For example, associate democracy with a roller coaster. Apply the elements of democracy to your school.

4. *Analyze*—Determine which element, if left out, would be most missed in a democracy.

5. *Evaluate*—Tell how people who live in a democracy might have a different existence than those who do not.

6. *Create*—Design a new form of government that would be safe and provide equity for people.

Principals can use this cubing activity with teachers as well, to help staff build their understanding of cognitive processes and the topics of differentiation. For example:

1. Identify an aspect of differentiation.

2. Summarize your understanding of a differentiated classroom.

3. Apply one thing you could use to differentiate.

4. Analyze whether or not your classroom supports differentiation.

5. Evaluate the positive and negative aspects of a differentiated classroom.

6. Create a differentiated learning activity.

Summary

Solid curriculum design and assessment practices provide the foundation for differentiated instruction. Backward planning from identified essential learning standards gives teachers the focus they need to ensure that students are working toward the same goals, even when the instructional practices teachers use to help students achieve mastery differ. Preassessment, assessment during learning, and assessment after learning ensure that instructional techniques have been effective, and teachers can use these data to revise their instructional practices.

Reflections for Principals

1. Do teachers examine the standards and determine the most essential learning?

2. Do teachers design their units of study backward from the standards?

3. Are students clear about the expectations—knowledge, concepts, and skills?

4. Do teachers use a variety of preassessments so they can be more precise with content and instruction?

5. Do teachers use formative assessments daily to adjust learning and regroup students?

6. Do teachers use tiered assignments?

7. Do students receive adequate feedback from their teacher and peers?

8. Do students have choices about how they show what they know?

FIVE
TEACHING IN THE DIFFERENTIATED CLASSROOM

It is the teacher's challenge to accommodate individual learner differences within the context of the classroom, and the principal's responsibility to support and encourage teachers in this process by helping them build an understanding of how they can implement strategies for differentiation within their daily routine. It is important to remember that differentiation is a process—not a one-step implementation—that involves recognizing the diversity of student needs, preassessing prior knowledge, strategically planning to meet student needs, and then evaluating how successful learning tasks were in helping all students achieve the learning.

According to Tomlinson (1999a), the following principles are key to instruction in the differentiated classroom:

- The teacher is clear about what the students should know, understand, and be able to do in the subject content.

- The teacher recognizes, appreciates, and builds on student differences.

- The teacher uses assessment and instruction in a reciprocal fashion.

- The teacher adjusts content, process, and product in response to student readiness, interests, and learning profile.

- Students participate in respectful work.

- Students and teachers are collaborators in learning.

- Maximum growth and success are goals of a differentiated classroom.

- Flexibility is key both when grouping students and when responding to their needs.

The classroom routine should flow in a sequence of teacher instruction, student grouping, and whole-class sharing that provides structure, aids the teacher in classroom management, and provides for opportunities to differentiate instruction.

Developing a Repertoire of Teaching Strategies

Differentiated instruction involves using a variety of instructional processes and engaging strategies that will intrigue the learner and help him or her persist in the learning to achieve mastery. Teachers must provide students with multiple tasks to rehearse their learning in ways that support students' sensory styles and multiple intelligences. This involves the following types of strategies:

- *Direct instruction*—A teacher-centered strategy in which the teacher presents new learning to students, often when covering a large quantity of material

- *Inquiry-based learning*—A student-centered strategy that requires students to conduct investigations independent of the teacher, unless otherwise guided through the discovery process

- *Cooperative learning*—A strategy based on grouping small teams of students heterogeneously according to ability, interest, and background

- *Information processing*—Strategies that teach students techniques for processing information so they can strategically organize, store, retrieve, and apply information; examples include using K-W-L charts, reciprocal teaching, graphic organizing, and webbing

Appropriate activities require students to develop and apply knowledge in ways that make sense to them and that they find meaningful and relevant, which takes into account student learning preferences and multiple intelligences. They also involve a variety of formative assessments that provide students with the opportunity to demonstrate their learning, such as projects, presentations, and exhibitions.

Choosing Strategies

Nine specific strategies for differentiation have been proven to increase student percentile gains in all subject disciplines, from kindergarten through grade 12 (Marzano et al., 2001). Following are the nine strategies and the corresponding brain research that supports each strategy.

1. *Identifying similarities and differences, comparing, contrasting, classifying, and using analogies and metaphors:* The brain needs to seek patterns, connections, and relationships between and among prior and new learning.

2. *Taking notes and summarizing:* The brain pays attention to meaningful information and deletes that which is not important.

3. *Reinforcing effort and providing recognition:* The brain responds to challenge and not to threat. Emotions enhance learning.

4. *Assigning homework and practice:* The popular phrase, "If you don't use it, you lose it," is true. Practice and rehearsal make learning stick.

5. *Generating nonlinguistic representations:* People recall visual stimuli with 90 percent accuracy.

6. *Using cooperative group learning:* The brain is social. Collaboration facilitates understanding and higher-order thinking.

7. *Setting objectives and providing feedback:* The brain responds to high challenge and continues to strive based on feedback.

8. *Generating and testing hypotheses:* The brain is curious and has an innate need to make meaning through patterns.

9. *Providing questions, cues, and advance organizers:* The brain responds to wholes and parts. All learners need to open "mental files" into which new learning can be stored.

These strategies support how the brain makes sense of new concepts and skills, engages, rehearses, and stores new learning. Figure 5.1 lists these strategies and links them to specific tactics teachers can use in the classroom.

Table 5.1: The Nine Instructional Strategies and Suggested Tactics for Classroom Instruction

Instructional Strategies	Tactics

Using similarities and differences, comparing, contrasting, classifying, and using analogies and metaphors	• Classifying
	• Comparing and contrasting
	  ▪ Venn diagrams
	  ▪ Synectics
	  ▪ Concept attainment
	  ▪ Concept formation

Note taking and summarizing	• Mind maps • Concept webs • Jigsaw • Reciprocal teaching • Templates and advance organizers
Reinforcing effort and providing recognition	• Giving feedback • Reflecting • Journaling • Making portfolios • Celebrating successes • Sharing stories of determination
Assigning homework and practice	• Extension of application • Four squares • Book bags • Puppets • 5-finger writing

continued →

Instructional Strategies	Tactics
Generating nonlinguistic representations	• Mind maps • Graphic organizers • Models
Using cooperative group learning	• Shared reading • Guided reading • Reciprocal learning • Peer editing • Buddy reading • Choral reading • Progressive writing • Jigsaw • Literature circles • Think-pair-share
Setting objectives and providing feedback	• Goal setting • Rubrics • Clear criteria • High expectations • Appropriate challenge and choice • Specific teacher, peer, and self-reflective feedback
Generating and testing hypotheses	• Research papers • Investigations • Debates • Persuasive writing • Portfolios • Case studies
Providing questions, cues, and advance organizers	• Agenda maps • Guided reading • Diagrams and charts • Graphic organizers • Wait time

Sources: Adapted from Gregory and Kuzmich, 2004; Gregory and Parry, 2006; and Marzano et al., 2001.

Developing Teachers' Use of Strategies

Principals must help teachers fill their toolkits with a variety of instructional strategies that have high payoff in student learning. As teachers become more comfortable with a full range of strategies that offer differentiation, they become more instructionally intelligent about selecting and using strategies that address student preferences and learning styles.

Marzano, Frontier, and Livingston (2011) note there are four levels of implementation regarding how effectively the strategy is used. Table 5.2 shows the levels of implementation and the characteristics of each stage.

Table 5.2: Four Levels of Implementation

Stages	Characteristics
Beginning	Little fluency, prone to errors, often with simplistic or inappropriate expectations
Developing	More precision, fewer errors, with an ease of use and appropriate complexity for students
Applying	Relative ease of use with no errors, with monitoring of students' reactions, probing, and refining student thinking
Innovating	Adapts the strategy for student needs and adds extensions when required

Source: Marzano et al., 2011.

Principals can model these instructional strategies themselves with content for teachers and then ask teachers to brainstorm how they can use the same strategies with their students. For example, at a faculty meeting the teachers may use a Venn diagram to look at similarities and differences between a traditional classroom and a differentiated classroom; then the group members could brainstorm how they could use a Venn diagram in the classroom. Principals can use think-pair-share with teachers and discuss the benefits and impact on learning, and then encourage teachers to use it in their classrooms to increase dialogue and check for understanding. Teachers could then bring back examples of work students created using the strategy to share with the group. A process such as this keeps the focus on instruction with little risk of challenging teachers' competence or self-image by applying a safe amount of pressure and support to encourage teachers to increase their repertoire of instructional strategies. This is not a mandate but rather a genuine effort to help teachers develop new approaches. Teachers would then share and discuss the samples and use one another as resources, celebrating their achievements (and the achievements of their students) along the way. Staff members represent a vast resource of expertise within each building. Principals should tap into this resource by encouraging teachers to share their expertise as they gain confidence.

Principals can also ask teachers to use a checklist, such as one similar to table 5.1 (page 53), to examine what tactics they are using in their classroom routinely with their students. This will give teachers and leaders a big picture of which strategies teachers are using consistently and which ones need to be added to teachers' toolkits.

Many other resources are available that outline specific tactics to help teachers fill their toolkits with best practices. One such resource is *Classroom Instruction That Works* (Marzano et al., 2001). Principals can facilitate whole-school or individual team book studies in which teachers examine instructional resources on a deep level.

Using Flexible Grouping

Flexible grouping is an integral part of the differentiated classroom, as students move in and out of the larger group and into partner, small-group, and independent work to tackle different tasks, such as processing, editing, problem solving, working on projects, and so on.

Gregory and Kaufeldt (2012) identify four specific types of groups utilized in the differentiated classroom: total, independent, partner, and small group (TIPS). In the total-class grouping, students are all doing the same thing, and the teacher is providing whole-class instruction. During independent work, all students are working on their own, engaged in a variety of tasks based on their interests, readiness, or choices. In partner work, students work with another student they choose, a student chosen randomly, a student chosen by the teacher, or a student who has a similar or opposite interest or skill (such as when one student is skilled in a task whereas another student is not, or when students have matching skill levels and the challenge is appropriate for both). In small-group work, student groups are based on interest or task or skill development (homogeneous or heterogeneous), or are randomly structured by the teacher or students. Table 5.3 provides suggested tactics for each type of group work.

Table 5.3: TIPS for Grouping Students in the Differentiated Classroom

Type of Group	Definition	Suggested Tactics
T: Total	The teacher is conducting whole-class instruction or all students are doing the same thing.	• Preassessing • Presenting new information • Demonstrating new skills • Observing a DVD • Participating in a jigsaw • Prereading text
I: Independent	All students are working independently on a variety of tasks based on interest, readiness, or choice.	• Preassessing • Journaling or creating portfolios • Self-assessing • Working on an independent study • Taking notes and summarizing • Reflecting • Creating exit cards
P: Partner	Students work with a partner selected through: • Random pairing • Teacher selection • Student choice • Task or interest	• Brainstorming • Processing information • Checking homework • Checking comprehension • Editing • Researching • Working on similar interests • Planning for homework

| S: Small group | Groups are interest or task oriented and structured in one of the following ways:

• Homogeneous for skill development

• Heterogeneous for skill development or diversity

• Random or structured by teacher or students | • Solving problems
• Working on group projects
• Working in learning centers
• Group learning assignments
• Conferencing about portfolios
• Investigating in groups
• Brainstorming |

Source: Adapted from Gregory and Kaufeldt, 2012.

As principals walk through classrooms, they should observe teacher's use of fluid groups—groups forming and reforming. Teachers should use on-the-spot observation and data to group students as needed. There should be a balance of teacher and students talking as well as student-to-student interaction and teacher interaction in the classroom. During walkthroughs, the principal can use the strategy of leaving a sticky note on the teacher's desk giving one compliment and asking one question about what he or she observed.

Using Technology in the Classroom

The students of the 21st century have always known electronic communication and had instant access to information on the Internet. Technology is as natural to them as breathing. They share a set of "net generation norms" (Tapscott, 2009):

- They need freedom to choose and to express themselves.

- They know how to explore the Internet.

- They are comfortable with and expect interactive experiences and learning.

- They are used to rapid communication, real-time chats, and responses.

- They want the latest technology and consistently seek innovative ways to collaborate, entertain themselves, work, and learn.

Thus, providing only traditional instruction with textbooks and lectures is unrealistic for 21st century learners; not only will it not meet their diverse needs, but it may also dampen their spirits and engagement in learning. The use of technology changes classroom instruction in multiple ways. It impacts both delivery of instruction—the strategies teachers use with students—and how students are grouped for instruction. For example:

- *Technology is multidimensional*—Students may simultaneously work on individual or group projects designed at several different readiness levels. This may serve both high- and low-ability students, as well as accommodate different learner styles (visual, kinesthetic, and auditory).

- *Technology enhances simultaneity*—Students become self-directed learners. Individual learners may pursue their goals independently while simultaneously using different applications. For example, computers can provide reteaching and enrichment as needed.

- *Technology increases immediacy*—Students can quickly move through basic skill and knowledge levels, thus increasing the amount of instructional time devoted to problem solving or higher-level thinking. This can support high-ability learners; however, students who need increased repetition of basic knowledge or skills also can be accommodated through technology. Simulations or other applications can be repeated numerous times until the concept is mastered.

- *Technology introduces unpredictability*—Students have the opportunity to solve problems in new and unexpected ways because of the numerous resources available through technology and the ability to communicate with others in real time.

Technology can support a differentiated classroom in many ways. By using networking capabilities, schools can provide students with learning opportunities that are independent of time and location. For example, students can participate in online courses for subjects not offered at the school, and homebound students are able to participate in schooling through applications such as Skype.

Technology can teach a concept in several different ways, catering to learner differences (such as visual, auditory, or kinesthetic). For example, a math computer program might show students a problem while also reading it to them and instructing them on how to use a manipulative to solve the problem. Students can also use technology to construct different elements of a project, such as by researching on the Internet, preparing a presentation using PowerPoint, and then producing an accompanying written report with computer-illustrated charts.

Technology can stimulate students to explore areas of interest in ways that were not possible in the past; it assists students in becoming self-directed learners. The Internet offers endless opportunities for students to research, exposes them to local and global collaboration opportunities, and gives them easy access to educational resources.

Students can use technology as a support for the work they do at home. Many schools have set up chat rooms on their websites where teachers offer homework help. Likewise, technology can facilitate home-to-school communication. Electronic communication—email, texts, and school web pages, to name a few—allows schools to communicate directly to parents, which can help teachers and parents regularly confer about student assignments, progress, and learning strategies.

Principals can assist teachers in using technology in their classrooms by helping them set personal goals related to using technology to support differentiation. Table 5.4 shows the stages of technology adoption in classrooms and their characteristics (Sandholtz, Ringstaff, & Dwyer, 2000), which are based on research conducted in Apple's Classroom of Tomorrow

Table 5.4: Stages of Technology Adoption in Classrooms

Stages	Characteristics
Entry	The teacher is in the planning stage of technology implementation and is not currently using technology for differentiation.
Adoption	Students use keyboarding skills and word-processing programs for writing assignments. There is some use of computer software programs for drill and practice of basic skills (not integrated into instruction).
Adaptation	Students compose work on computers. Many basic instructional activities are self-paced and individualized using technology. Teaching is changing or evolving because of increases in student productivity and teacher use of technology.
Appropriation	The teacher is experimenting with interdisciplinary or project-based instruction. There is an increased instructional focus on higher-order thinking skills and how technology can support their development. The teacher may also be experimenting with team teaching or student collaboration using technology and will be considering adopting new assessment strategies that incorporate technology.
Invention	The teacher meets or exceeds instructional goals with technology. He or she uses technology to support higher-order thinking as part of an integrated curriculum. The teacher demonstrates a balance between direct teaching and project-based learning using a variety of technologies (the Internet, data collection, data analysis, and presentation). The teacher has integrated or is integrating alternative assessments that involve technology.

Source: Adapted from Sandholtz et al., 2000.

project. Principals can use these stages to evaluate (during classroom observations) teachers' progress in using technology to support differentiated instruction. Classrooms in which teachers use technology to support differentiated instruction will likely be in the later stages (appropriation and invention).

Avoiding Classroom-Management Issues

One area of concern that often causes teachers to abandon differentiation is classroom management. Because of the flexibility and fluidity of the differentiated classroom, teachers often fear that chaos will ensue if they begin implementing a variety of activities and expect students to work in groups. They worry about students being off task and creating distractions.

Teachers in differentiated classrooms should do the following to keep students on task and organized and help them be self-directed and sufficient:

- Make directions for all activities accessible for all students. If teachers share directions orally only, students may forget them. Directions and steps should be printed or posted so students can check what to do next.

- Make directions and materials available for students to access independently. Consider color coding each step to help students find their place. Laminated agenda sheets help keep students on track while in learning centers.

- Encourage students to work together and collaborate to achieve clarification.

- Give students individual contracts or agendas so they have a choice of the order in which they do tasks. Some students prefer to do things that interest them first, while others want to do their least favorite task first to get it out of the way.

- Brainstorm with students about "what to do if you don't know what to do" so they understand ways to help themselves and their peers solve problems. Post a chart with the group's ideas that students can reference when needed.

In addition, establishing routines for when students come into the classroom helps students get and stay focused. *Anchors* are tasks that help students focus and eliminate distracters at the beginning of class. Teachers should design anchors carefully to ensure activities or tasks relate to the curriculum objectives, allow for rehearsal of key concepts and skills, are interesting and engaging, are worthy of the time spent (not just fillers), and are encouraging. Such anchor tasks might include working with a partner to review homework or solving a problem that covers skills learned in the previous class.

To avoid classroom management problems, teachers must also have tasks that keep students busy. These *sponges* are tasks that "soak up time." Because students and groups finish tasks at different rates, teachers must provide challenges or extensions to fill in the time. As with anchors, these tasks should be meaningful and reinforce learning goals—they should not just be busy work or fun, although it's great if the work is both enjoyable and purposeful. Such tasks might include:

- Creating a crossword puzzle of key vocabulary words

- Drawing a mind map to summarize learning

- Journaling about a topic or concept

- Working on a portfolio or a culminating assignment

- Working in the student's choice of station or center

Supporting Teachers

Even though teachers have the primary responsibility when it comes to implementing differentiated instruction in the classroom, principals play a critical role. They can support teachers in the following ways.

Establish Partnerships

Establishing strong partnerships is key to implementing successful educational change. Teachers need opportunities and time to consult and plan with each other. Collaboration might include general education teachers working together or with specialists, special education teachers, or gifted education teachers. It is important to provide regular and uninterrupted planning time and to recognize that teachers need time to learn to work together for the benefit of students (Watts & Castle, 1993, cited in Corcoran, 1995).

Teachers also need access to ample materials that provide a continuum of resources for academically diverse classrooms. One size does not fit all in a differentiated classroom. There must be an investment in curricular materials that provide different levels of challenge and appeal to different learning styles and interests. Principals should also support the discovery of new ways of using the curriculum. Curriculum specialists should work with teachers and provide instructional support as needed (Tomlinson, 1999b).

Teachers and principals need to partner to ensure that the overall school environment supports differentiated instruction. Partnering may include limiting the overload on teachers, providing ample planning time, offering incentives for innovation in the classroom, and reviewing or changing policies and procedures that limit differentiation (Tomlinson, 1999b).

Support New Teachers

Principals should pay special attention to supporting new teachers. During their first year of teaching, many novice teachers report struggling with time for lesson planning, a perceived lack of administrative support, and a shortage of materials and resources. They are concerned with simply surviving the basics of lesson planning; they see differentiation as yet another hurdle. Principals, however, can provide them with resources and support their growth. Consider how you support novice teachers in your school: Do you regularly visit their classrooms to offer encouragement? Do you provide specific time for them to consult with more experienced teachers who differentiate instruction? Taking the time to offer encouragement and allowing time for new teachers to observe and meet with teachers who differentiate instruction is critical. Making easy-to-understand and practical resources about differentiation available to these teachers is also helpful.

Model Differentiation

Principals should consider the importance of role modeling in establishing educational practice. Model the concepts of differentiation with staff in faculty meetings; study staff learning styles and structure meetings to appeal to a variety of learners, for example. Principals should recognize that, like students, teachers have different levels of readiness, and their goals should be personalized to account for this. Provide support based on teachers' individual needs. Ensure that staff development opportunities address a wide range of teaching abilities and readiness levels. Consider evaluating teachers on how they set and achieve goals for differentiation in the classroom. In other words, apply the principles of differentiated instruction schoolwide (Gregory, 2008).

Encourage Teachers to Start Small, but Think Big

Just as students need time to progress toward mastery, so do teachers. Teachers can start small by becoming familiar with differentiation by reviewing a variety of resources and materials, using partners to process the information, trying out new techniques in the classroom, and then reteaching in small groups. Table 5.5 (page 62) gives some suggestions for a process of implementing differentiated instruction.

Table 5.5: Sample Three-Stage Implementation

Getting Started	Moving Along	More Advanced
Collect a variety of resources and reading materials. Use partners to process (using think-pair-share). Vary instructional strategies. Reteach in small groups.	Use small groups. Vary complexity of tasks and pacing. Use quick preassessments, graphic organizers, and rubrics. Offer choices. Engage interest groups.	Use tiered assignments, tiered centers, contracts, choice boards, research-based instructional strategies, agendas, and contracts.

Principals can then lead discussion about where staff members are along the continuum of implementation. Create a chart, such as the one in Table 5.6, to reflect on current practice and future goals.

Table 5.6: My Current Practice and Future Goals

What Am I Doing Already?	What Do I Want to Do Next Semester?	What Do I Want to Do Long Term?

Summary

In the differentiated classroom, teachers are clear about what students should know, understand, and be able to do; they appreciate and build on student differences; they adjust content, process, and product in response to students' individual needs; and they engage students in collaborative processes in which flexibility is key. This promotes maximum student growth and success. Principals can support teachers as they implement differentiation by helping them form partnerships, providing extra guidance for new teachers, modeling differentiation, and helping teachers get started—no matter how small the initial effort.

Reflections for Principals

1. Is there a pattern in how teachers provide instruction? Is there small-group work, independent work, and work with partners, or do teachers use whole-group instruction only?

2. Is there time for whole-class sharing?

3. Do teachers give students the opportunity to select their assignments or learning experiences?

4. How is technology being used by teachers? Do teachers embed the use of technology in their lesson plans?

5. Do teachers use technology to differentiate instruction? Do they use it for repetition, practice, and drill, or for collaborative projects and research?

6. How can you encourage teachers to devote time to planning for differentiated instruction?

7. How can you support professional development that encourages differentiated instruction?

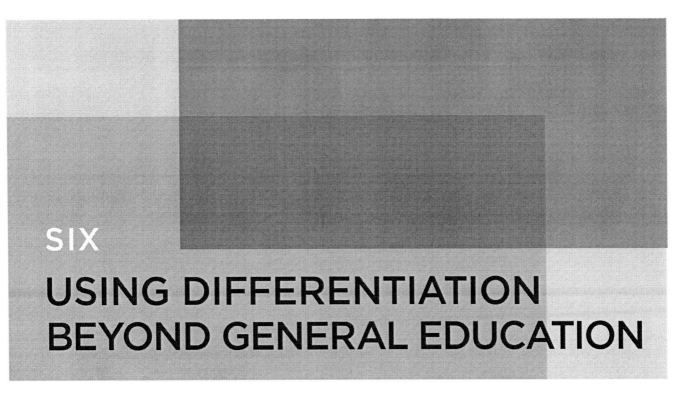

SIX

USING DIFFERENTIATION BEYOND GENERAL EDUCATION

Differentiated classrooms provide multilevel instruction and multiple teaching strategies to engage learners with varying interest and ability levels in the general education classroom. Differentiation is also a best practice for learners with special needs, gifted learners, learners with attention difficulties, and English learners (ELs).

Learners With Special Needs

Learners with special needs are eligible for services under the federal Individuals with Disabilities Education Act (IDEA), which was reauthorized in 2004 to align with the federal No Child Left Behind legislation. IDEA requires that every eligible child have an Individualized Education Program (IEP), which requires developing individual learning goals and identifying appropriate accommodations for each eligible student.

Central to IDEA is the practice of *inclusion*—"providing specially designed instruction and supports for students with disabilities and special education needs within the context of the general education settings" (Patterson, 2001, p. 43). This means including students with special needs in classrooms with general education students whenever possible. Interestingly, the instructional practices needed to support inclusion are similar to those used in differentiated classrooms. Patterson (2001) shares the following practices:

- *Specially designed instruction*—For example, teachers in differentiated classrooms demonstrate flexibility in learning activities, homework assignments, and testing procedures that can address all learners, including those with special needs.

- *Multilevel instruction*—Differentiation calls for preassessing students' prior knowledge and providing instruction that suits individual student needs.

- *Collaboration among students*—Differentiation calls for using various strategies for student grouping, such as partner work and small-group work, and involves using instructional tactics, such as peer review, that call for collaboration among students.

- *Support for individual learning differences*—Differentiation is all about providing learning opportunities that support a broad range of student learning preferences and students' multiple intelligences.

- *Collaboration between special educators and classroom teachers*—General education teachers can seek out the opinions of special education teachers to discover which strategies and techniques might work for students with special needs in the regular classroom. Special education teachers often have more time to know individual learners and more opportunities to experiment with strategies one on one with students.

Response to Intervention and Differentiation

The 2004 IDEA reauthorization promotes the use of the response to intervention (RTI) model to identify and meet the learning needs of struggling students. Designed as a prevention model, the RTI process uses three tiers of support and intervention to ensure student mastery of learning goals:

- *Tier 1*—Classroom teachers provide general instruction that varies in the following ways: content, process, time, and scaffolding—according to students' needs.

- *Tier 2*—Students receive small-group instruction to build their skills toward targeted standards.

- *Tier 3*—Students receive additional intensive interventions if they do not make progress toward mastering skills with the interventions in Tier 2.

In all the tiers of RTI, teachers use research-based, proven strategies to assess learners and ensure that they master content. This intervention model designed for prevention may reduce a school's need for special education referrals.

Gifted Learners

In general, gifted students are those whose aptitude and performance surpass the standard for children of the same age (Reber & Reber, 2001). Because these students quickly master grade-level material, teachers may not focus their instruction on their needs. As a result, these students often do not reach their potential and sometimes even exhibit problems in the regular classroom. They may become bored with repetitive tasks that they have already mastered. They may become disenchanted with learning and disengaged if they are not challenged. Gifted students deserve to be challenged so they can work to and fulfill their potential.

Differentiated instruction allows teachers to focus on these students and provide them with challenging assignments based on their level of prior knowledge and mastery. For example, tiering assignments for complexity and depth of understanding provides opportunity for enrichment beyond the regular curriculum for gifted learners. Assignments that include investigation and research in a gifted student's area of interest or passion are engaging for the student and provide opportunity for choice. The Triarchic Model (Sternberg, 1985) suggests that students will become more successfully intelligent if they not only know information but can be analytical, practical, and creative with the knowledge. They may also be more intrigued with learning if it is approached from an analytical, a practical, and a creative way.

There is one subset of gifted learners who are often overlooked: those who have a high aptitude and average or below-average performance. These students often do poorly in some subjects and extremely well in others (Butler-Por, 1993). Gifted students with learning difficulties are often misunderstood and thus underserved by the educational system. Differentiated classrooms can be an effective way of providing support for these students. Consider the following teaching strategies.

- If reading is an issue, find other ways to help the student understand the material. Some options include photographs, films, audio books, and parent or peer tutors.

- If organization is an issue, teach the student to use some formal organization system, such as outlines, study guides, a syllabus of topics, visual aids, timelines, folders, or a color-key organization system. If the student has trouble using a conventional outline style, try webbing or mind mapping.

- If a student gets bogged down by letter formation or spelling while writing, allow the student to type assignments on a computer. This way the student can complete assignments that otherwise he or she might not be able to complete or that might take so long as to cause frustration.

- If a student exhibits verbal processing issues and has trouble communicating his or her ideas verbally, find ways to communicate besides writing. Some alternatives include models, speeches, mime, acting, murals, films, posters, drawings, charts, and demonstrations.

- If short-term memory is an issue for a student, use strategies that compensate. For example, if the student has a poor auditory memory and has difficulty remembering assignments given verbally, ask him or her to write down the assignments or use pictures as cues. If the student has trouble with verbal memory, teach him or her to use mnemonics or visualization techniques (Baum, 1990).

Learners With Attention Difficulties

Differentiating instruction also benefits students with attention difficulties. According to Welton (1999), there are three identified types of attention difficulties:

1. Some students have problems with *arousal* and subsequently experience frequent fatigue or drowsiness, an inability to stay on task, indifference to classroom transitions, and slowness in responding to stimuli.

2. Some students experience problems with *selective attention*. These students are easily distracted, have trouble identifying main points of reading materials, make careless mistakes, and may be disorganized.

3. Some students have difficulties with *divided attention*. These students may have problems performing more than one task at a time or tasks that involve multiple steps. They also may experience trouble following multipart directions.

Students with arousal problems may benefit from shorter lessons, auditory or visual cues to announce transitions, and color in materials. Students with selective attention may benefit from classroom strategies that use prompts to focus attention. They may also benefit when teachers remind them to proofread their work, teach organizational strategies, and allow them to work with a peer. Students with divided attention thrive with simplified directions, when teachers break down tasks into component parts, and when they are allowed to use audio and video recording as a form of note taking.

Note that these strategies can be adopted easily in differentiated classrooms and, though designed for students with attention difficulties, would be of benefit to all learners. Many instructional techniques used in the differentiated classroom benefit learners with attention difficulties and do not require any modification from teachers for use with these learners. Some possibilities include the following:

- Providing charts or menus with steps and directions for reference during work tasks

- Providing a quiet place in the classroom where students can go to retreat

- Using color coding and symbols to help students organize materials

English Learners

The multilevel assignments and multiple strategies used in a differentiated classroom can provide ELs with options for assignments that teach content while improving language skills through vocabulary building, reading comprehension, and writing exercises. Assigning ELs to small groups or pairing them with a capable peer allows students to hear vocabulary and language patterns and to speak in a low-risk environment with one or several others. This interaction allows them to mirror their peers and develop vocabulary and understanding of the concepts or skills being explored. Giving students many opportunities to practice speaking and developing their vocabulary further as an embedded part of the learning process is important. Additionally, many EL teachers are adept at personalizing instruction and are valuable resources for both the principal and the general education teacher when planning instruction to include ELs (see also Gregory & Burkman, 2012).

Summary

Differentiation allows teachers to better help all their students succeed—this includes general education students as well as those with unique learning needs, such as learners with special needs, gifted learners, learners with attention difficulties, and English learners—by providing multiple levels of instruction and multiple teaching strategies to engage students with varying interest and ability levels.

Reflections for Principals

1. How do teachers use differentiation to support students with special needs?

2. Are gifted students benefiting from differentiated instruction? Are they being challenged and enriched in the regular classroom?

3. Do teachers use differentiated instruction to support students with attention difficulties and help them stay focused and engaged?

4. Do teachers differentiate instruction in ways that help English learners further develop their oral and written language development?

EPILOGUE
LEADING WITH DIFFERENTIATION

The very best teachers in our schools have similar qualities. As DuFour and Eaker (1998) note, teachers have a contagious enthusiasm. They have a clear sense of what they want to accomplish. They know how to communicate in students' terms. They believe in students and give students confidence. They are passionate about teaching. They never give up—they are tenacious. They are tremendous motivators. They are challenging, but they make it fun to meet the challenge. They are energizing; students like to be around them. According to Haselkorn and Harris (1998), these teachers are also trained well and are knowledgeable about effective teaching, have a thorough grasp of the subject area, are able to foster good relationships with students, understand how the brain works and makes memory, connect with parents as collaborators, are respectful of the uniqueness of each learner, and are knowledgeable about child development.

Teachers need ongoing practice and support from the principal and other administrators to build these skills of the very best teachers. Teachers need encouragement to not only try a new strategy or approach but to continue to use the strategy in a variety of appropriate situations and refine it over time to fit student needs.

It is critical for principals to translate theory into practice when establishing new schoolwide patterns for educational practice. Principals can do this by providing staff development opportunities and remembering to hold teachers accountable for implementing the best practices they learn. By identifying teachers' individual needs and abilities—through many of the same strategies teachers use to create student learning profiles—and incorporating them into staff development plans, principals can help teachers get the most out of their instruction for differentiation (Gregory, 2008). A lack of consideration for how teachers learn new knowledge and skills may also be a reason why teachers have trouble integrating new knowledge and skills into their practice and often leave the profession. If administrators honor teachers' learning preferences, teachers are more able to respect the differences in how their students learn.

Teachers will be at various stages along the differentiation learning continuum, so staff development should be based on teacher readiness and interests. Principals should offer different choices and paths to follow. Some teachers may prefer a book study. Others might like online courses, webinars, conferences, peer planning, observation, or mentoring, to name a few.

It is important to define key terms and develop a common language in which to speak about differentiated instruction. It is also important to allow time for teachers to process, practice, and refine their skills. The more sustained practice teachers have with support from their colleagues, the greater the level of implementation. Respecting teachers' efforts and sharing and celebrating successes at faculty meetings reinforces the concept, keeps the focus on differentiation, and allows ideas and strategies to "cross pollinate" so all teachers benefit from the experiences of others.

Get teachers talking about the rationale for differentiation. Principals can do this by using book, article, or video studies; mentoring; coaching; using action research; examining student work; analyzing data; and doing case studies. Capture teachers' attention and stimulate their learning in a variety of ways during staff development and meetings. Begin meetings in interesting and novel ways. Use technology, visuals, and graphics. Model differentiation by using multiple strategies for instruction that are appealing to teachers with different learning styles and preferences. Some examples for activities to get teachers talking about differentiation include the following:

- Show two contrasting video clips—one that shows students who are disengaged (such as the scene in *Ferris Bueller's Day Off* in which the teacher presents a boring, unengaging monologue about the Great Depression) and one that shows students engaged in learning (such as a scene from *Stand and Deliver* or *Dead Poets Society*). Have the teachers jot down all the reasons the students are disengaged as they watch the first video clip and ask them to suggest more brain-compatible ways to have students interact with the information. Then analyze the positive clip and ask teachers to note why the teaching works and whether differentiation is evident.

- Present neuroscience or brain research with an article, such as *The Art of Changing the Brain* (Zull, 2002), and ask teachers to create a mind map of things the brain likes and what we know about the uniqueness of learners.

- Ask teachers to share with one another what was important to them as learners in their classrooms when they were students. Who was the greatest teacher and why?

- Ask teachers to write about the following topic: "If I had a child or (grandchild) in our school, what kind of classroom would I want them to be in every day?" Encourage the use of vivid description and specific ideas.

Differentiated instruction is a way for teachers to capture learners' attention in engaging and intriguing ways with low risk and an appropriate level of challenge. When principals model this same type of instruction with their staff members by respecting and accommodating diversity, teachers are much more likely to practice the same in their classrooms. One size does not fit all for adult learners or young students.

This resource is intended to help principals build their knowledge base about differentiated instruction so they can support and encourage their teachers, share information with stakeholders, and ultimately foster increased student success. Research into best practice shows that differentiated instruction can lead to success for all students—those in general education classrooms, students with special needs, gifted students, students with attention difficulties, and English learners. Principals must help their teachers understand and develop their skills in differentiation so students are the beneficiaries.

REFERENCES AND RESOURCES

Allington, R. L., & Cunningham, P. M. (2007). *Schools that work: Where all children read and write* (3rd ed.). Boston: Pearson.

Anderson, L. W., & Krathwohl, D. R. (Eds.). (2001). *A taxonomy for learning, teaching, and assessing: A revision of Bloom's taxonomy of educational objectives* (Complete ed.). New York: Longman.

Aronson, E. (1978). *The jigsaw classroom.* Beverly Hills, CA: SAGE.

Arroyo, A. A., Rhoad, R., & Drew, P. (1999). Meeting diverse student needs in urban schools: Research-based recommendations for school personnel. *Preventing School Failure, 43*(4), 145–153.

Baum, S. (1990). *Gifted but learning disabled: A puzzling paradox.* Washington, DC: Office of Educational Research and Improvement.

Berk, L. E. (2000). *Child development* (5th ed.). Boston: Allyn & Bacon.

Berte, N. R. (Ed.). (1975). *Individualizing education by learning contracts.* San Francisco: Jossey-Bass.

Black, P., & Wiliam, D. (2009). Developing the theory of formative assessment. *Educational Assessment, Evaluation and Accountability, 21*(1), 5–31.

Blakemore, S.-J., & Frith, U. (2005). *The learning brain: Lessons for education.* Malden, MA: Blackwell.

Bloom B. S. (1956). *Taxonomy of educational objectives, handbook I: The cognitive domain.* New York: David McKay.

Bridgeland, J. M., DiIulio, J. J., & Morison, K. B. (2006). *The silent epidemic: Perspectives of high school dropouts.* Washington, DC: Civic Enterprises.

Brooks, J. G., & Brooks, M. G. (1993). *In search of understanding: The case for constructivist classrooms.* Alexandria, VA: Association for Supervision and Curriculum Development.

Brooks, R., & Goldstein, S. (2008). The mindset of teachers capable of fostering resilience in students. *Canadian Journal of School Psychology, 23*(1), 114–126.

Butler-Por, N. (1993). Underachieving gifted students. In K. A. Heller & F. J. Mönks (Eds.), *International handbook of research and development of giftedness and talent* (pp. 649–668). New York: Pergamon Press.

Caine, R. N., & Caine, G. (1994). *Making connections: Teaching and the human brain.* Reading, MA: Addison-Wesley.

Corcoran, T. B. (1995). *Helping teachers teach well: Transforming professional development* (CPRE Policy Brief). Philadelphia: Consortium for Policy Research in Education.

Cowan, G., & Cowan, E. (1980). *Writing.* New York: Wiley.

Csikszentmihalyi, M. (1990). *Flow: The psychology of optimal experience.* New York: Harper & Row.

Csikszentmihalyi, M., Rathunde, K., & Whalen, S. (1993). *Talented teenagers: The roots of success and failure.* New York: Cambridge University Press.

Damasio, A. R. (1994). *Descartes' error: Emotion, reason and the human brain.* New York: Putnam.

Damasio, A. (2003). *Looking for Spinoza: Joy, sorrow, and the feeling brain.* Orlando, FL: Harcourt.

Deschenes, C., Ebeling, D. G., & Sprague, J. (1994). *Adapting curriculum & instruction in inclusive classrooms: A teacher's desk reference.* Bloomington, IN: The Center for School and Community Integration, Institute for the Study of Developmental Disabilities.

DuFour, R., & Eaker, R. (1998). *Professional learning communities at work: Best practices for enhancing student achievement.* Bloomington, IN: National Educational Service.

Dunn, R., & Dunn, K. (1992). *Teaching elementary students through their individual learning styles: Practical approaches for grades 3–6.* Boston: Allyn & Bacon.

Dweck, C. S. (2006). *Mindset: The new psychology of success.* New York: Random House.

Educational Research Service. (1998). *Enhancing student engagement in learning.* Arlington, VA: Author.

Frederiksen, J. R., & Collins, A. (1989). A systems approach to educational testing. *Educational Researcher, 18*(9), 27–32.

Friends Western School. (n.d.). *Multiple intelligence inventory.* Accessed at http://friendswesternschool.org/resources/mii.pdf on March 1, 2012.

Gardner, H. (1983). *Frames of mind: The theory of multiple intelligences.* New York: Basic Books.

Gardner, H. (1999). *Intelligence reframed: Multiple intelligences for the 21st century.* New York: Basic Books.

Gardner, H. (2006). *Multiple intelligences: New horizons.* New York: Basic Books.

Geake, J. G. (2009). *The brain at school: Educational neuroscience in the classroom.* Berkshire, UK: Open University Press.

Geary, D. C. (1998). *Male, female: The evolution of human sex differences.* Washington, DC: American Psychological Association.

Georgia Department of Education. (2003). *Differentiated instruction planning sheet.* Accessed at www.glc.k12.ga.us/passwd/trcl/ttools/attach/pdc/DiffInstPlanSheet.pdf.

Gibbs, J. (2006). *Reaching all by creating tribes learning communities.* Windsor, CA: CenterSource Systems.

Gordon, W. J. J. (1961). *Synectics: The development of creative capacity.* New York: Harper.

Grant, J. (2003). Differentiating for diversity. *Principal, 82*(3), 48–51.

Gregorc, A. F. (1985). *Inside styles: Beyond the basics: Questions and answers on style.* Maynard, MA: Gabriel Systems.

Gregory, G. H. (2005). *Differentiating instruction with style.* Thousand Oaks, CA: Corwin Press.

Gregory, G. H. (2008). *Differentiated instructional strategies in practice: Training, implementation, and supervision* (2nd ed.). Thousand Oaks, CA: Corwin Press.

Gregory, G. H., & Burkman, A. (2012). *Differentiated literacy strategies for English language learners, grades K–6.* Thousand Oaks, CA: Corwin Press.

Gregory. G. H., & Chapman, C. (2007). *Differentiated instructional strategies: One size doesn't fit all* (2nd ed.). Thousand Oaks, CA: Corwin Press.

Gregory, G., & Kaufeldt, M. (2012). *Think big, start small: How to differentiate instruction in a brain-friendly classroom.* Bloomington, IN: Solution Tree Press.

Gregory, G. H., & Kuzmich, L. (2004). *Data driven differentiation in the standards-based classroom.* Thousand Oaks, CA: Corwin Press.

Gregory, G. H., & Kuzmich, L. (2007). *Teacher teams that get results: 61 strategies for sustaining and renewing professional learning communities.* Thousand Oaks, CA: Corwin Press.

Gregory, G. H., & Kuzmich, L. (2010). *Student teams that get results: Teaching tools for the differentiated classroom.* Thousand Oaks, CA: Corwin Press.

Gregory, G. H., & Parry, T. (2006). *Designing brain-compatible learning* (3rd ed.). Thousand Oaks, CA: Corwin Press.

Gurian, M., Henley, P., & Trueman, T. (2001). *Boys and girls learn differently: A guide for teachers and parents.* San Francisco: Jossey-Bass.

Hallowell, E. M. (2011). *Shine: Using brain science to get the best from your people.* Boston: Harvard Business School.

Halpern, D. F. (2000). *Sex differences in cognitive abilities* (3rd ed.). Mahwah, NJ: Erlbaum.

Haselkorn, D., & Harris, L. (1998). *The essential profession: A national survey of public attitudes toward teaching, educational opportunity, and school reform.* Belmont, MA: Recruiting New Teachers.

Hord, S. M., Rutherford, W. L., Huling-Austin, L., & Hall, G. E. (1987). *Taking charge of change.* Alexandria, VA: Association of Supervision and Curriculum Development.

Hoy, A. W., & Hoy, W. K. (2003). *Instructional leadership: A learning-centered guide.* New York: Allyn & Bacon.

Jenkins, J. M., & Keefe, J. W. (2001). Strategies for personalizing instruction: A typology for improving teaching and learning. *NASSP Bulletin, 85*(629), 72–82.

Johnson, L. M. (2003). *What we know about: Culture and learning.* Arlington, VA: Educational Research Service.

Jonassen, D. H., & Grabowski, B. L. (1993). *Handbook of individual differences, learning, and instruction.* Hillsdale, NJ: Erlbaum.

Jones, C. F. (1994). *Mistakes that worked: 40 familiar inventions and how they came to be.* New York: Doubleday.

Jones, C. F. (1996). *Accidents may happen.* New York: Delacorte Press.

Kagan, S. (1994). *Cooperative learning.* San Clemente, CA: Kagan.

Kagan, S., & Kagan, M. (1998). *Multiple intelligences: The complete MI book.* San Clemente, CA: Kagan.

Kandel, E. R., Schwartz, J. H., & Jessell, T. M. (2000). *Principles of neural science* (4th ed.). New York: McGraw-Hill.

Kapusnick, R. A., & Hauslein, C. M. (2001). The "silver cup" of differentiated instruction. *Kappa Delta Pi Record, 37*(4), 156–159.

Keefe, J. W., & Jenkins, J. M. (2002). Personalized instruction. *Phi Delta Kappan, 83*(6), 440–448.

Knowles, M. S. (1986). *Using learning contracts.* San Francisco: Jossey-Bass.

Kolb, D. A. (1984). *Experiential learning: Experience as the source of learning and development.* Englewood Cliffs, NJ: Prentice Hall.

LeDoux, J. (2002). *Synaptic self: How our brains become who we are.* New York: Viking.

Linn, M. C., & Peterson, A. C. (1985). Emergence and characterization of sex differences in spatial ability: A meta-analysis. *Child Development, 56*(6), 1479–1498.

Marzano, R. J. (2003). *What works in schools: Translating research into action.* Alexandria, VA: Association for Supervision and Curriculum Development.

Marzano, R. J., Frontier, A., & Livingston, D. (2011). *Effective supervision: Supporting the art and science of teaching.* Alexandria, VA: Association for Supervision and Curriculum Development.

Marzano, R. J., Pickering, D. J., & Pollock, J. E. (2001). *Classroom instruction that works: Research-based strategies for increasing student achievement.* Alexandria VA: Association for Supervision and Curriculum Development.

McCarthy, B., & McCarthy, D. (2006). *Teaching around the 4MAT cycle: Designing instruction for diverse learners with diverse learning styles.* Thousand Oaks, CA: Corwin Press.

Medina, J. (2008). *Brain rules: 12 Principles for surviving and thriving at work, home, and school.* Seattle, WA: Pear Press.

Medina, J. (2010). *Brain rules for baby.* Seattle, WA: Pear Press.

National Association of Advisers and Inspectors in Design and Technology. (1996). *Meeting the individual needs of all pupils in design and technology at key stages 3–4.* Daventry UK: Author.

National Center for Learning Disabilities. (2009). *What are learning disabilities?* Accessed at www
.ncld.org/ld-basics/ld-explained/basic-facts/what-are-learning-disabilities on May 25, 2012.

National Study of School Evaluation. (1997). *Indicators of schools of quality* (Vol. 1.). Schaumburg, IL:
Author.

Orkwis, R., & McLane, K. (1998). *A curriculum every student can use: Design principles for student
access* (ERIC/OSEP Topical Brief). Reston, VA: The ERIC Clearinghouse on Disabilities and
Gifted Education.

Ornestein, A. C., & Hunkins, F. P. (1998). *Curriculum: Foundations, principles, and issues* (3rd ed.).
Boston: Allyn & Bacon.

Panksepp, J. (2004). *Affective neuroscience: The foundations of human and animal emotions.* New York:
Oxford University Press.

Page, S. W. (2000). When changes for the gifted spur differentiation for all. *Educational Leadership,
58*(1), 62–65.

Paterson, K. (1977). *Bridge to Terabithia.* New York: Crowell.

Patterson, J. (2001). *School leader's guide to special education: Essentials for principals.* Alexandria,
VA: National Association of Elementary School Principals.

Posen, D. B. (1995). *Stress management for patient and physician.* Accessed at www.mentalhealth
.com/mag1/p51-str.html on August 23, 2011.

Posner, M. I., & Rothbart, M. K. (2007). *Educating the human brain.* Washington, DC: American
Psychological Association.

Protheroe, N. (2001). *Meeting the challenges of high-stakes testing: Essentials for principals.* Alexandria,
VA: National Association of Elementary School Principals.

Radius, M., & Lesniak, P. (1997). *Student success teams: Supporting teachers in general education.*
Sacramento: California Department of Education.

Ramsay, H. (1991). Reinventing the wheel? A review of the development and performance of
employee involvement. *Human Resource Management Journal, 1*(4), 1–22.

Ratey, J. (2008). *Spark: The revolutionary new science of exercise and the brain.* New York: Little, Brown.

Reber, A. S., & Reber, E. S. (2001). *The Penguin dictionary of psychology* (3rd ed.). London: Penguin.

Reis, S. M., & Renzulli, J. S. (1992). Using curriculum compacting to challenge the above-average.
Educational Leadership, 50(2), 51–57.

Rogers, E. M. (1995). *Diffusion of innovations* (4th ed.). New York: Free Press.

Rogoff, B. (1998). Cognition as collaborative process. In W. Damon, R. M. Lerner, D. Kuhn, & R. S.
Siegler (Eds.), *Handbook of child psychology: Cognition, perception and language* (Vol. 2, 5th ed.,
pp. 679–144). New York: Wiley.

Sandholtz, J. H., Ringstaff, C., & Dwyer, D. C. (1997). *Teaching with technology: Creating student-centered classrooms.* New York: Teachers College Press.

Sandholtz, J. H., Ringstaff, C., & Dwyer, D. C. (2000). The evolution of instruction in technology-rich classrooms. In *The Jossey-Bass Reading on Technology and Learning* (pp. 225–276). San Francisco: Jossey-Bass.

Shaw, P., Greenstein, D., Lerch, J., Clasen, L., Lenroot, R., Gogtay, N., et al. (2006). Intellectual ability and cortical development in children and adolescents. *Nature, 440*(7084), 676–679.

Shellard, E. (2002). *Urban principals respond: For the good of the children: Professional development for principals and teachers.* Alexandria, VA: National Association of Elementary School Principals.

Sileo, T. W., & Prather, M. A. (1998). Creating classroom environments that assess the linguistic and cultural backgrounds of students with disabilities: An Asian Pacific American perspective. *Remedial and Special Education, 19*(6), 323–337.

Silver, H. F., Strong, R. W., & Perini, M. J. (2000). *So each may learn: Integrating learning styles and multiple intelligences.* Alexandria, VA: Association for Supervision and Curriculum Development.

Sousa, D., & Tomlinson, C. A. (2011). *Differentiation and the brain: How neuroscience supports the learner-friendly classroom.* Bloomington, IN: Solution Tree Press.

Sternberg, R. J. (1985). *Beyond IQ: A triarchic theory of human intelligence.* New York: Cambridge University Press.

Sternberg, R. J., Torff, B., & Grigorenko, E. L. (1998). Teaching triarchically improves school achievement. *Journal of Educational Psychology, 90*(3), 374–384.

Sullivan, M. (1996). A meta-analysis of experimental research studies based on the Dunn and Dunn learning styles model and its relationship to academic achievement. *National Forum of Applied Educational Research Journal, 10*(1).

Tapscott, D. (2009). *Grown up digital: How the net generation is changing your world.* New York: McGraw-Hill.

Teachnology Incorporated. (2011). *How to differentiate instruction.* Accessed at www.teach-nology.com/tutorials/teaching/differentiate on January 24, 2012.

Tomlinson, C. A. (1995). *How to differentiate instruction in mixed-ability classrooms.* Alexandria, VA: Association for Supervision and Curriculum Development.

Tomlinson, C. A. (1999a). *The differentiated classroom: Responding to the needs of all learners.* Alexandria, VA: Association for Supervision and Curriculum Development.

Tomlinson, C. A. (1999b). Leadership for differentiated classrooms. *School Administrator, 56*(9), 6–11.

Tomlinson, C. A., & Eidson, C. C. (2003). *Differentiation in practice: A resource guide for differentiating curriculum.* Alexandria, VA: Association for Supervision and Curriculum Development.

U.S. Department of Education. (1992). *Hard work and high expectations: Motivating students to learn.* Accessed at www.kidsource.com/kidsource/content3/work.expectations.k12.4.html on August 24, 2011.

Vallecorsa, A. L., deBettencourt, L. U., & Zigmond, N. (2000). *Students with mild disabilities in general education settings: A guide for special educators.* Upper Saddle River, NJ: Merrill.

Vygotsky, L. S. (1978). *Mind in society: The development of higher psychological processes.* Cambridge, MA: Harvard University Press.

Weber, C. L., Colarulli-Daniels, R., & Leinhauser, J. A. (2003). A tale of two principals. *Gifted Child Today, 26*(4), 55–62.

Wehrmann, K. S. (2000). Baby steps: A beginner's guide. *Educational Leadership, 58*(1), 20–23.

Welton, E. N. (1999). How to help inattentive students find success in school: Getting the homework back from the dog. *Teaching Exceptional Children, 31*(6), 12–18.

Wig, G. S., Grafton, S. T., Demos, K. E., & Kelley, W. M. (2005). Reductions in neural activity underlie behavioral components of repetition priming. *Nature Neuroscience, 8*(9), 1228–1233.

Wiggins, G. (1998). *Educative assessment: Designing assessments to inform and improve student performance.* San Francisco: Jossey-Bass.

Wiggins, G., & McTighe, J. (1998). *Understanding by design.* Alexandria, VA: Association for Supervision and Curriculum Development.

Willard-Holt, C. (1999). *Dual exceptionalities* (ERIC Digest E574). Reston, VA: ERIC Clearinghouse on Disabilities and Gifted Education.

Willingham, W. W., & Cole, N. S. (1997). *Gender and fair assessment.* Mahwah, NJ: Erlbaum.

Willis, J. (2006). *Research-based strategies to ignite student learning: Insights from a neurologist and a classroom teacher.* Alexandria, VA: Association for Supervision and Curriculum Development.

Willis, J. (2007). *Brain-friendly strategies for the inclusion classroom.* Alexandria, VA: Association of Supervision and Curriculum Development.

Willis, J. (2008). *How your child learns best: Brain-friendly strategies you can use to ignite your child's learning and increase school success.* Naperville, IL: Sourcebooks.

Willis, J. (2010, May 9). Want children to "pay attention"? Make their brains curious! [Web log post]. Accessed at www.psychologytoday.com/blog/radical-teaching/201005/want-children-pay-attention-make-their-brains-curious on August 24, 2011.

Winebrenner, S. (1992). *Teaching gifted kids in the regular classroom: Strategies and techniques every teacher can use to meet the academic needs of the gifted and talented.* Minneapolis, MN: Free Spirit.

Zull, J. E. (2002). *The art of changing the brain: Enriching teaching by exploring the biology of learning.* Sterling, VA: Stylus.